W9-CMO-466

Flask Web Development

Miguel Grinberg

Beijing · Cambridge · Farnham · Köln · Sebastopol · Tokyo

Flask Web Development

by Miguel Grinberg

Published by O'Reilly Media, Inc., 1005 Gravenstein Highway North, Sebastopol, CA 95472.

O'Reilly books may be purchased for educational, business, or sales promotional use. Online editions are also available for most titles (*http://my.safaribooksonline.com*). For more information, contact our corporate/institutional sales department: 800-998-9938 or *corporate@oreilly.com*.

Editors: Meghan Blanchette and Rachel Roumeliotis
Production Editor: Nicole Shelby
Copyeditor: Nancy Kotary
Proofreader: Charles Roumeliotis

Cover Designer: Randy Comer
Interior Designer: David Futato
Illustrator: Rebecca Demarest

May 2014:   First Edition

Revision History for the First Edition:

2014-04-25:   First release

See *http://oreilly.com/catalog/errata.csp?isbn=9781449372620* for release details.

ISBN: 978-1-449-37262-0

[LSI]

For Alicia.

Table of Contents

Part II.   Example: A Social Blogging Application

Part III.   The Last Mile

Preface

Flask stands out from other frameworks because it lets developers take the driver's seat and have full creative control of their applications. Maybe you have heard the phrase "fighting the framework" before. This happens with most frameworks when you decide to solve a problem with a solution that isn't the official one. It could be that you want to use a different database engine, or maybe a different method of authenticating users. Deviating from the path set by the framework's developers will give you lots of headaches.

Flask is not like that. Do you like relational databases? Great. Flask supports them all. Maybe you prefer a NoSQL database? No problem at all. Flask works with them too. Want to use your own homegrown database engine? Don't need a database at all? Still fine. With Flask you can choose the components of your application or even write your own if that is what you want. No questions asked!

The key to this freedom is that Flask was designed from the start to be extended. It comes with a robust core that includes the basic functionality that all web applications need and expects the rest to be provided by some of the many third-party extensions in the ecosystem and, of course, by you.

In this book I present my workflow for developing web applications with Flask. I don't claim to have the only true way to build applications with this framework. You should take my choices as recommendations and not as gospel.

Most software development books provide small and focused code examples that demonstrate the different features of the target technology in isolation, leaving the "glue" code that is necessary to transform these different features into a fully working applications to be figured out by the reader. I take a completely different approach. All the examples I present are part of a single application that starts out very simple and is expanded in each successive chapter. This application begins life with just a few lines of code and ends as a nicely featured blogging and social networking application.

Who This Book Is For

You should have some level of Python coding experience to make the most of this book. Although the book assumes no previous Flask knowledge, Python concepts such as packages, modules, functions, decorators, and object-oriented programming are assumed to be well understood. Some familiarity with exceptions and diagnosing issues from stack traces will be very useful.

While working through the examples in this book, you will spend a great deal of time in the command line. You should feel comfortable using the command line of your operating system.

Modern web applications cannot avoid the use of HTML, CSS, and JavaScript. The example application that is developed throughout the book obviously makes use of these, but the book itself does not go into a lot of detail regarding these technologies and how they are used. Some degree of familiarity with these languages is recommended if you intend to develop complete applications without the help of a developer versed in client-side techniques.

I released the companion application to this book as open source on GitHub. Although GitHub makes it possible to download applications as regular ZIP or TAR files, I strongly recommend that you install a Git client and familiarize yourself with source code version control, at least with the basic commands to clone and check out the different versions of the application directly from the repository. The short list of commands that you'll need is shown in "How to Work with the Example Code " on page xiii. You will want to use version control for your own projects as well, so use this book as an excuse to learn Git!

Finally, this book is not a complete and exhaustive reference on the Flask framework. Most features are covered, but you should complement this book with the official Flask documentation (*http://flask.pocoo.org*).

How This Book Is Organized

This book is divided into three parts:

Part I, Introduction to Flask, explores the basics of web application development with the Flask framework and some of its extensions:

- Chapter 1 describes the installation and setup of the Flask framework.
- Chapter 2 dives straight into Flask with a basic application.
- Chapter 3 introduces the use of templates in Flask applications.
- Chapter 4 introduces web forms.
- Chapter 5 introduces databases.

- Chapter 6 introduces email support.
- Chapter 7 presents an application structure that is appropriate for medium and large applications.

Part II, Example: A Social Blogging Application, builds Flasky, the open source blogging and social networking application that I developed for this book:

- Chapter 8 implements a user authentication system.
- Chapter 9 implements user roles and permissions.
- Chapter 10 implements user profile pages.
- Chapter 11 creates the blogging interface.
- Chapter 12 implements followers.
- Chapter 13 implements user comments for blog posts.
- Chapter 14 implements an Application Programming Interface (API).

Part III, The Last Mile, describes some important tasks not directly related to application coding that need to be considered before publishing an application:

- Chapter 15 describes different unit testing strategies in detail.
- Chapter 16 gives an overview of performance analysis techniques.
- Chapter 17 describes deployment options for Flask applications, both traditional and cloud based.
- Chapter 18 lists additional resources.

How to Work with the Example Code

The code examples presented in this book are available from GitHub at *https://github.com/miguelgrinberg/flasky*.

The commit history in this repository was carefully created to match the order in which concepts are presented in the book. The recommended way to work with the code is to check out the commits starting from the oldest, then move forward through the commit list as you make progress with the book. As an alternative, GitHub will also let you download each commit as a ZIP or TAR file.

If you decide to use Git to work with the source code, then you need to install the Git client, which you can download from *http://git-scm.com*. The following command downloads the example code using Git:

```
$ git clone https://github.com/miguelgrinberg/flasky.git
```

The `git clone` command installs the source code from GitHub into a *flasky* folder that is created in the current directory. This folder does not contain just source code; a copy of the Git repository with the entire history of changes made to the application is also included.

In the first chapter you will be asked to *check out* the initial release of the application, and then, at the proper places you will be instructed to move forward in the history. The Git command that lets you move through the change history is `git checkout`. Here is an example:

```
$ git checkout 1a
```

The `1a` referenced in the command is a *tag*, a named point in the history of the project. This repository is tagged according to the chapters of the book, so the `1a` tag used in the example sets the application files to the initial version used in Chapter 1. Most chapters have more than one tag associated with them, so, for example, tags `5a`, `5b`, and so on are incremental versions presented in Chapter 5.

In addition to checking out the source files for a version of the application, you may need to perform some setup. For example, in some cases you will need to install additional Python packages or apply updates to the database. You will be told when these are necessary.

You will normally not modify the source files of the application, but if you do, then Git will not let you check out a different revision, as that would cause your local changes to be lost. Before you can check out a different revision, you will need to revert the files to their original state. The easiest way to do this is with the `git reset` command:

```
$ git reset --hard
```

This command will destroy your local changes, so you should save anything you don't want to lose before you use this command.

From time to time, you may want to refresh your local repository from the one on GitHub, where bug fixes and improvements may have been applied. The commands that achieve this are:

```
$ git fetch --all
$ git fetch --tags
$ git reset --hard origin/master
```

The `git fetch` commands are used to update the commit history and the tags in your local repository from the remote one on GitHub, but none of this affects the actual source files, which are updated with the `git reset` command that follows. Once again, be aware that any time `git reset` is used you will lose any local changes you have made.

Another useful operation is to view all the differences between two versions of the application. This can be very useful to understand a change in detail. From the command line, the `git diff` command can do this. For example, to see the difference between revisions 2a and 2b, use:

```
$ git diff  2a 2b
```

The differences are shown as a *patch*, which is not a very intuitive format to review changes if you are not used to working with patch files. You may find that the graphical comparisons shown by GitHub are much easier to read. For example, the differences between revisions 2a and 2b can be viewed on GitHub at *https://github.com/miguelgrin berg/flasky/compare/2a...2b*

Using Code Examples

This book is here to help you get your job done. In general, if example code is offered with this book, you may use it in your programs and documentation. You do not need to contact us for permission unless you're reproducing a significant portion of the code. For example, writing a program that uses several chunks of code from this book does not require permission. Selling or distributing a CD-ROM of examples from O'Reilly books does require permission. Answering a question by citing this book and quoting example code does not require permission. Incorporating a significant amount of example code from this book into your product's documentation does require permission.

We appreciate, but do not require, attribution. An attribution usually includes the title, author, publisher, and ISBN. For example: "*Flask Web Development* by Miguel Grinberg (O'Reilly). Copyright 2014 Miguel Grinberg, 978-1-449-3726-2."

If you feel your use of code examples falls outside fair use or the permission given above, feel free to contact us at *permissions@oreilly.com*.

Conventions Used in This Book

The following typographical conventions are used in this book:

Italic
> Indicates new terms, URLs, email addresses, filenames, and file extensions.

`Constant width`
> Used for program listings, as well as within paragraphs to refer to program elements such as variable or function names, databases, data types, environment variables, statements, and keywords.

`Constant width bold`
> Shows commands or other text that should be typed literally by the user.

Constant width italic
> Shows text that should be replaced with user-supplied values or by values determined by context.

 This element signifies a tip or suggestion.

 This element signifies a general note.

 This element indicates a warning or caution.

Safari® Books Online

 Safari Books Online is an on-demand digital library that delivers expert content in both book and video form from the world's leading authors in technology and business.

Technology professionals, software developers, web designers, and business and creative professionals use Safari Books Online as their primary resource for research, problem solving, learning, and certification training.

Safari Books Online offers a range of product mixes and pricing programs for organizations, government agencies, and individuals. Subscribers have access to thousands of books, training videos, and prepublication manuscripts in one fully searchable database from publishers like O'Reilly Media, Prentice Hall Professional, Addison-Wesley Professional, Microsoft Press, Sams, Que, Peachpit Press, Focal Press, Cisco Press, John Wiley & Sons, Syngress, Morgan Kaufmann, IBM Redbooks, Packt, Adobe Press, FT Press, Apress, Manning, New Riders, McGraw-Hill, Jones & Bartlett, Course Technology, and dozens more. For more information about Safari Books Online, please visit us online.

How to Contact Us

Please address comments and questions concerning this book to the publisher:

O'Reilly Media, Inc.
1005 Gravenstein Highway North
Sebastopol, CA 95472
800-998-9938 (in the United States or Canada)
707-829-0515 (international or local)
707-829-0104 (fax)

We have a web page for this book, where we list errata, examples, and any additional information. You can access this page at *http://www.bit.ly/flask-web-dev*.

To comment or ask technical questions about this book, send email to *bookques tions@oreilly.com*.

For more information about our books, courses, conferences, and news, see our website at *http://www.oreilly.com*.

Find us on Facebook: *http://facebook.com/oreilly*

Follow us on Twitter: *http://twitter.com/oreillymedia*

Watch us on YouTube: *http://www.youtube.com/oreillymedia*

Acknowledgments

I could not have written this book alone. I have received a lot of help from family, co-workers, old friends, and new friends I've made along the way.

I'd like to thank Brendan Kohler for his detailed technical review and for his help in giving shape to the chapter on Application Programming Interfaces. I'm also in debt to David Baumgold, Todd Brunhoff, Cecil Rock, and Matthew Hugues, who reviewed the manuscript at different stages of completion and gave me very useful advice regarding what to cover and how to organize the material.

Writing the code examples for this book was a considerable effort. I appreciate the help of Daniel Hofmann, who did a thorough code review of the application and pointed out several improvements. I'm also thankful to my teenage son, Dylan Grinberg, who suspended his Minecraft addiction for a few weekends and helped me test the code under several platforms.

O'Reilly has a wonderful program called Early Release that allows impatient readers to have access to books while they are being written. Some of my Early Release readers went the extra mile and engaged in useful conversations regarding their experience working through the book, leading to significant improvements. I'd like to acknowledge

Sundeep Gupta, Dan Caron, Brian Wisti and Cody Scott in particular for the contributions they've made to this book.

The staff at O'Reilly Media has always been there for me. Above all I'd like to recognize my wonderful editor, Meghan Blanchette, for her support, advice, and assistance from the very first day we met. Meg has made the experience of writing my first book a memorable one.

To conclude, I would like to give a big thank you to the awesome Flask community.

Introduction to Flask

## CHAPTER 1

Installation

Flask (*http://flask.pocoo.org/*) is a small framework by most standards, small enough to be called a "micro-framework." It is small enough that once you become familiar with it, you will likely be able to read and understand all of its source code.

But being small does not mean that it does less than other frameworks. Flask was designed as an extensible framework from the ground up; it provides a solid core with the basic services, while *extensions* provide the rest. Because you can pick and choose the extension packages that you want, you end up with a lean stack that has no bloat and does exactly what you need.

Flask has two main dependencies. The routing, debugging, and Web Server Gateway Interface (WSGI) subsystems come from Werkzeug (*http://werkzeug.pocoo.org/*), while template support is provided by Jinja2 (*http://jinja.pocoo.org/*). Werkzeug and Jinja2 are authored by the core developer of Flask.

There is no native support in Flask for accessing databases, validating web forms, authenticating users, or other high-level tasks. These and many other key services most web applications need are available through extensions that integrate with the core packages. As a developer, you have the power to cherry-pick the extensions that work best for your project or even write your own if you feel inclined to. This is in contrast with a larger framework, where most choices have been made for you and are hard or sometimes impossible to change.

In this chapter, you will learn how to install Flask. The only requirement you need is a computer with Python installed.

 The code examples in this book have been verified to work with Python 2.7 and Python 3.3, so using one of these two versions is strongly recommended.

Using Virtual Environments

The most convenient way to install Flask is to use a virtual environment. A virtual environment is a private copy of the Python interpreter onto which you can install packages privately, without affecting the global Python interpreter installed in your system.

Virtual environments are very useful because they prevent package clutter and version conflicts in the system's Python interpreter. Creating a virtual environment for each application ensures that applications have access to only the packages that they use, while the global interpreter remains neat and clean and serves only as a source from which more virtual environments can be created. As an added benefit, virtual environments don't require administrator rights.

Virtual environments are created with the third-party *virtualenv* utility. To check whether you have it installed in your system, type the following command:

```
$ virtualenv --version
```

If you get an error, you will have to install the utility.

 Python 3.3 adds native support of virtual environments through the venv module and the pyvenv command. pyvenv can be used instead of virtualenv, but note that virtual environments created with pyvenv on Python 3.3 do not include pip, which needs to be installed manually. This limitation has been removed in Python 3.4, where pyvenv can be used as a complete virtualenv replacement.

Most Linux distributions provide a package for virtualenv. For example, Ubuntu users can install it with this command:

```
$ sudo apt-get install python-virtualenv
```

If you are using Mac OS X, then you can install virtualenv using easy_install:

```
$ sudo easy_install virtualenv
```

If you are using Microsoft Windows or any operating system that does not provide an official virtualenv package, then you have a slightly more complicated install procedure.

Using your web browser, navigate to *https://bitbucket.org/pypa/setuptools*, the home of the setuptools installer. In that page, look for a link to download the installer script. This is a script called *ez_setup.py*. Save this file to a temporary folder on your computer, then run the following commands in that folder:

```
$ python ez_setup.py
$ easy_install virtualenv
```

The previous commands must be issued from an account with administrator rights. On Microsoft Windows, start the command prompt window using the "Run as Administrator" option. On Unix-based systems, the two installation commands must be preceded with sudo or executed as the root user. Once installed, the virtualenv utility can be invoked from regular accounts.

Now you need to create the folder that will host the example code, which is available from a GitHub repository. As discussed in "How to Work with the Example Code " on page xiii, the most convenient way to do this is by checking out the code directly from GitHub using a Git client. The following commands download the example code from GitHub and initialize the application folder to version "1a," the initial version of the application:

```
$ git clone https://github.com/miguelgrinberg/flasky.git
$ cd flasky
$ git checkout 1a
```

The next step is to create the Python virtual environment inside the *flasky* folder using the virtualenv command. This command has a single required argument: the name of the virtual environment. A folder with the chosen name will be created in the current directory and all files associated with the virtual environment will be inside. A commonly used naming convention for virtual environments is to call them *venv*:

```
$ virtualenv venv
New python executable in venv/bin/python2.7
Also creating executable in venv/bin/python
Installing setuptools...........done.
Installing pip..............done.
```

Now you have a *venv* folder inside the *flasky* folder with a brand-new virtual environment that contains a private Python interpreter. To start using the virtual environment, you have to "activate" it. If you are using a bash command line (Linux and Mac OS X users), you can activate the virtual environment with this command:

```
$ source venv/bin/activate
```

If you are using Microsoft Windows, the activation command is:

```
$ venv\Scripts\activate
```

When a virtual environment is activated, the location of its Python interpreter is added to the PATH, but this change is not permanent; it affects only your current command session. To remind you that you have activated a virtual environment, the activation command modifies the command prompt to include the name of the environment:

```
(venv) $
```

When you are done working with the virtual environment and want to return to the global Python interpreter, type `deactivate` at the command prompt.

Installing Python Packages with pip

Most Python packages are installed with the *pip* utility, which virtualenv automatically adds to all virtual environments upon creation. When a virtual environment is activated, the location of the pip utility is added to the PATH.

 If you created the virtual environment with pyvenv under Python 3.3, then pip must be installed manually. Installation instructions are available on the pip website (*http://bit.ly/pip-install*). Under Python 3.4, pyvenv installs pip automatically.

To install Flask into the virtual environment, use the following command:

```
(venv) $ pip install flask
```

With this command, Flask and its dependencies are installed in the virtual environment. You can verify that Flask was installed correctly by starting the Python interpreter and trying to import it:

```
(venv) $ python
>>> import flask
>>>
```

If no errors appear, you can congratulate yourself: you are ready for the next chapter, where you will write your first web application.

## CHAPTER 2

Basic Application Structure

In this chapter, you will learn about the different parts of a Flask application. You will also write and run your first Flask web application.

Initialization

All Flask applications must create an *application instance*. The web server passes all requests it receives from clients to this object for handling, using a protocol called Web Server Gateway Interface (WSGI). The application instance is an object of class Flask, usually created as follows:

```
from flask import Flask
app = Flask(__name__)
```

The only required argument to the Flask class constructor is the name of the main module or package of the application. For most applications, Python's __name__ variable is the correct value.

The *name* argument that is passed to the Flask application constructor is a source of confusion among new Flask developers. Flask uses this argument to determine the root path of the application so that it later can find resource files relative to the location of the application.

Later you will see more complex examples of application initialization, but for simple applications this is all that is needed.

Routes and View Functions

Clients such as web browsers send *requests* to the web server, which in turn sends them to the Flask application instance. The application instance needs to know what code needs to run for each URL requested, so it keeps a mapping of URLs to Python functions. The association between a URL and the function that handles it is called a *route*.

The most convenient way to define a route in a Flask application is through the `app.route` decorator exposed by the application instance, which registers the decorated function as a route. The following example shows how a route is declared using this decorator:

```
@app.route('/')
def index():
    return '<h1>Hello World!</h1>'
```

 Decorators are a standard feature of the Python language; they can modify the behavior of a function in different ways. A common pattern is to use decorators to register functions as handlers for an event.

The previous example registers the function `index()` as the handler for the application's root URL. If this application were deployed on a server associated with the *www.example.com* domain name, then navigating to *http://www.example.com* on your browser would trigger `index()` to run on the server. The return value of this function, called the *response*, is what the client receives. If the client is a web browser, the response is the document that is displayed to the user.

Functions like `index()` are called *view functions*. A response returned by a view function can be a simple string with HTML content, but it can also take more complex forms, as you will see later.

 Response strings embedded in Python code lead to code that is difficult to maintain, and it is done here only to introduce the concept of responses. You will learn the proper way to generate responses in Chapter 3.

If you pay attention to how some URLs for services that you use every day are formed, you will notice that many have variable sections. For example, the URL for your Facebook profile page is *http://www.facebook.com/<your-name>*, so your username is part of it. Flask supports these types of URLs using a special syntax in the `route` decorator. The following example defines a route that has a dynamic name component:

```
@app.route('/user/<name>')
def user(name):
    return '<h1>Hello, %s!</h1>' % name
```

The portion enclosed in angle brackets is the dynamic part, so any URLs that match the static portions will be mapped to this route. When the view function is invoked, Flask sends the dynamic component as an argument. In the earlier example view function, this argument is used to generate a personalized greeting as a response.

The dynamic components in routes are strings by default but can also be defined with a type. For example, route /user/<int:id> would match only URLs that have an integer in the id dynamic segment. Flask supports types int, float, and path for routes. The path type also represents a string but does not consider slashes as separators and instead considers them part of the dynamic component.

Server Startup

The application instance has a run method that launches Flask's integrated development web server:

```
if __name__ == '__main__':
    app.run(debug=True)
```

The `__name__ == '__main__'` Python idiom is used here to ensure that the development web server is started only when the script is executed directly. When the script is imported by another script, it is assumed that the parent script will launch a different server, so the app.run() call is skipped.

Once the server starts up, it goes into a loop that waits for requests and services them. This loop continues until the application is stopped, for example by hitting Ctrl-C.

There are several option arguments that can be given to app.run() to configure the mode of operation of the web server. During development, it is convenient to enable debug mode, which among other things activates the *debugger* and the *reloader*. This is done by passing the argument debug set to True.

 The web server provided by Flask is not intended for production use. You will learn about production web servers in Chapter 17.

A Complete Application

In the previous sections, you learned about the different parts of a Flask web application, and now it is time to write one. The entire *hello.py* application script is nothing more than the three parts described earlier combined in a single file. The application is shown in Example 2-1.

Example 2-1. hello.py: A complete Flask application

```
from flask import Flask
app = Flask(__name__)

@app.route('/')
def index():
    return '<h1>Hello World!</h1>'

if __name__ == '__main__':
    app.run(debug=True)
```

 If you have cloned the application's Git repository on GitHub, you can now run `git checkout 2a` to check out this version of the application.

To run the application, make sure that the virtual environment you created earlier is activated and has Flask installed. Now open your web browser and type *http://127.0.0.1:5000/* in the address bar. Figure 2-1 shows the web browser after connecting to the application.

Figure 2-1. hello.py Flask application

Then launch the application with the following command:

```
(venv) $ python hello.py
 * Running on http://127.0.0.1:5000/
 * Restarting with reloader
```

If you type any other URL, the application will not know how to handle it and will return an error code 404 to the browser—the familiar error that you get when you navigate to a web page that does not exist.

The enhanced version of the application shown in Example 2-2 adds a second route that is dynamic. When you visit this URL, you are presented with a personalized greeting.

Example 2-2. hello.py: Flask application with a dynamic route

```python
from flask import Flask
app = Flask(__name__)

@app.route('/')
def index():
    return '<h1>Hello World!</h1>'

@app.route('/user/<name>')
def user(name):
    return '<h1>Hello, %s!</h1>' % name

if __name__ == '__main__':
    app.run(debug=True)
```

If you have cloned the application's Git repository on GitHub, you can now run `git checkout 2b` to check out this version of the application.

To test the dynamic route, make sure the server is running and then navigate to `http://localhost:5000/user/Dave`. The application will respond with a customized greeting, generated using the `name` dynamic argument. Try different names to see how the view function always generates the response based on the name given. An example is shown in Figure 2-2.

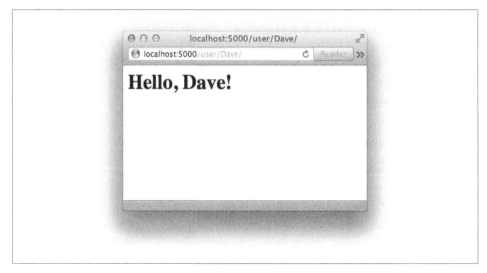

Figure 2-2. Dynamic route

The Request-Response Cycle

Now that you have played with a basic Flask application, you might want to know more about how Flask works its magic. The following sections describe some of the design aspects of the framework.

Application and Request Contexts

When Flask receives a request from a client, it needs to make a few objects available to the view function that will handle it. A good example is the *request object*, which encapsulates the HTTP request sent by the client.

The obvious way in which Flask could give a view function access to the request object is by sending it as an argument, but that would require every single view function in the application to have an extra argument. Things get more complicated if you consider that the request object is not the only object that view functions might need to access to fulfill a request.

To avoid cluttering view functions with lots of arguments that may or may not be needed, Flask uses *contexts* to temporarily make certain objects globally accessible. Thanks to contexts, view functions like the following one can be written:

```
from flask import request

@app.route('/')
def index():
```

```
user_agent = request.headers.get('User-Agent')
return '<p>Your browser is %s</p>' % user_agent
```

Note how in this view function `request` is used as if it was a global variable. In reality, `request` cannot be a global variable if you consider that in a multithreaded server the threads are working on different requests from different clients at the same time, so each thread needs to see a different object in `request`. Contexts enable Flask to make certain variables globally accessible to a thread without interfering with the other threads.

 A thread is the smallest sequence of instructions that can be managed independently. It is common for a process to have multiple active threads, sometimes sharing resources such as memory or file handles. Multithreaded web servers start a pool of threads and select a thread from the pool to handle each incoming request.

There are two contexts in Flask: the *application context* and the *request context*. Table 2-1 shows the variables exposed by each of these contexts.

Table 2-1. Flask context globals

Variable name	Context	Description
current_app	Application context	The application instance for the active application.
g	Application context	An object that the application can use for temporary storage during the handling of a request. This variable is reset with each request.
request	Request context	The request object, which encapsulates the contents of a HTTP request sent by the client.
session	Request context	The user session, a dictionary that the application can use to store values that are "remembered" between requests.

Flask activates (or *pushes*) the application and request contexts before dispatching a request and then removes them when the request is handled. When the application context is pushed, the `current_app` and `g` variables become available to the thread; likewise, when the request context is pushed, `request` and `session` become available as well. If any of these variables are accessed without an active application or request context, an error is generated. The four context variables will be revisited in later chapters in detail, so don't worry if you don't understand why they are useful yet.

The following Python shell session demonstrates how the application context works:

```
>>> from hello import app
>>> from flask import current_app
>>> current_app.name
Traceback (most recent call last):
...
RuntimeError: working outside of application context
```

```
>>> app_ctx = app.app_context()
>>> app_ctx.push()
>>> current_app.name
'hello'
>>> app_ctx.pop()
```

In this example, `current_app.name` fails when there is no application context active but becomes valid once a context is pushed. Note how an application context is obtained by invoking `app.app_context()` on the application instance.

Request Dispatching

When the application receives a request from a client, it needs to find what view function to invoke to service it. For this task, Flask looks up the URL given in the request in the application's *URL map*, which contains a mapping of URLs to the view functions that handle them. Flask builds this map using the `app.route` decorators or the equivalent nondecorator version `app.add_url_rule()`.

To see what the URL map in a Flask application looks like, you can inspect the map created for *hello.py* in the Python shell. For this test, make sure that your virtual environment is activated:

```
(venv) $ python
>>> from hello import app
>>> app.url_map
Map([<Rule '/' (HEAD, OPTIONS, GET) -> index>,
 <Rule '/static/<filename>' (HEAD, OPTIONS, GET) -> static>,
 <Rule '/user/<name>' (HEAD, OPTIONS, GET) -> user>])
```

The / and */user/<name>* routes were defined by the `app.route` decorators in the application. The */static/<filename>* route is a special route added by Flask to give access to static files. You will learn more about static files in Chapter 3.

The `HEAD, OPTIONS, GET` elements shown in the URL map are the *request methods* that are handled by the route. Flask attaches methods to each route so that different request methods sent to the same URL can be handled by different view functions. The `HEAD` and `OPTIONS` methods are managed automatically by Flask, so in practice it can be said that in this application the three routes in the URL map are attached to the `GET` method. You will learn about specifying different request methods for routes in Chapter 4.

Request Hooks

Sometimes it is useful to execute code before or after each request is processed. For example, at the start of each request it may be necessary to create a database connection, or authenticate the user making the request. Instead of duplicating the code that does this in every view function, Flask gives you the option to register common functions to be invoked before or after a request is dispatched to a view function.

Request hooks are implemented as decorators. These are the four hooks supported by Flask:

- `before_first_request`: Register a function to run before the first request is handled.
- `before_request`: Register a function to run before each request.
- `after_request`: Register a function to run after each request, if no unhandled exceptions occurred.
- `teardown_request`: Register a function to run after each request, even if unhandled exceptions occurred.

A common pattern to share data between request hook functions and view functions is to use the g context global. For example, a `before_request` handler can load the logged-in user from the database and store it in g.user. Later, when the view function is invoked, it can access the user from there.

Examples of request hooks will be shown in future chapters, so don't worry if this does not quite make sense yet.

Responses

When Flask invokes a view function, it expects its return value to be the response to the request. In most cases the response is a simple string that is sent back to the client as an HTML page.

But the HTTP protocol requires more than a string as a response to a request. A very important part of the HTTP response is the *status code*, which Flask by default sets to 200, the code that indicates that the request was carried out successfully.

When a view function needs to respond with a different status code, it can add the numeric code as a second return value after the response text. For example, the following view function returns a 400 status code, the code for a bad request error:

```
@app.route('/')
def index():
    return '<h1>Bad Request</h1>', 400
```

Responses returned by view functions can also take a third argument, a dictionary of headers that are added to the HTTP response. This is rarely needed, but you will see an example in Chapter 14.

Instead of returning one, two, or three values as a tuple, Flask view functions have the option of returning a `Response` object. The `make_response()` function takes one, two, or three arguments, the same values that can be returned from a view function, and returns a `Response` object. Sometimes it is useful to perform this conversion inside the view function and then use the methods of the response object to further configure the response. The following example creates a response object and then sets a cookie in it:

```
from flask import make_response

@app.route('/')
def index():
    response = make_response('<h1>This document carries a cookie!</h1>')
    response.set_cookie('answer', '42')
    return response
```

There is a special type of response called a *redirect*. This response does not include a page document; it just gives the browser a new URL from which to load a new page. Redirects are commonly used with web forms, as you will learn in Chapter 4.

A redirect is typically indicated with a 302 response status code and the URL to redirect to given in a Location header. A redirect response can be generated using a three-value return, or also with a Response object, but given its frequent use, Flask provides a redirect() helper function that creates this response:

```
from flask import redirect

@app.route('/')
def index():
    return redirect('http://www.example.com')
```

Another special response is issued with the abort function, which is used for error handling. The following example returns status code 404 if the id dynamic argument given in the URL does not represent a valid user:

```
from flask import abort

@app.route('/user/<id>')
def get_user(id):
    user = load_user(id)
    if not user:
        abort(404)
    return '<h1>Hello, %s</h1>' % user.name
```

Note that abort does not return control back to the function that calls it but gives control back to the web server by raising an exception.

Flask Extensions

Flask is designed to be extended. It intentionally stays out of areas of important functionality such as database and user authentication, giving you the freedom to select the packages that fit your application the best, or to write your own if you so desire.

There is a large variety of *extensions* for many different purposes that were created by the community, and if that is not enough, any standard Python package or library can be used as well. To give you an idea of how an extension is incorporated into an application, the following section adds an extension to *hello.py* that enhances the application with command-line arguments.

Command-Line Options with Flask-Script

Flask's development web server supports a number of startup configuration options, but the only way to specify them is by passing them as arguments to the `app.run()` call in the script. This is not very convenient; the ideal way to pass configuration options is through command-line arguments.

Flask-Script is an extension for Flask that adds a command-line parser to your Flask application. It comes packaged with a set of general-purpose options and also supports custom commands.

The extension is installed with pip:

```
(venv) $ pip install flask-script
```

Example 2-3 shows the changes needed to add command-line parsing to the *hello.py* application.

Example 2-3. hello.py: Using Flask-Script

```
from flask.ext.script import Manager
manager = Manager(app)

# ...

if __name__ == '__main__':
    manager.run()
```

Extensions developed specifically for Flask are exposed under the `flask.ext` namespace. Flask-Script exports a class named `Manager`, which is imported from `flask.ext.script`.

The method of initialization of this extension is common to many extensions: an instance of the main class is initialized by passing the application instance as an argument to the constructor. The created object is then used as appropriate for each extension. In this case, the server startup is routed through `manager.run()`, where the command line is parsed.

If you have cloned the application's Git repository on GitHub, you can run git checkout 2c to check out this version of the application.

With these changes, the application acquires a basic set of command-line options. Running *hello.py* now shows a usage message:

```
$ python hello.py
usage: hello.py [-h] {shell,runserver} ...

positional arguments:
  {shell,runserver}
    shell            Runs a Python shell inside Flask application context.
    runserver        Runs the Flask development server i.e. app.run()

optional arguments:
  -h, --help         show this help message and exit
```

The shell command is used to start a Python shell session in the context of the application. You can use this session to run maintenance tasks or tests, or to debug issues.

The runserver command, as its name implies, starts the web server. Running python hello.py runserver starts the web server in debug mode, but there many more options available:

```
(venv) $ python hello.py runserver --help
usage: hello.py runserver [-h] [-t HOST] [-p PORT] [--threaded]
                          [--processes PROCESSES] [--passthrough-errors] [-d]
                          [-r]

Runs the Flask development server i.e. app.run()

optional arguments:
  -h, --help             show this help message and exit
  -t HOST, --host HOST
  -p PORT, --port PORT
  --threaded
  --processes PROCESSES
  --passthrough-errors
  -d, --no-debug
  -r, --no-reload
```

The --host argument is a useful option because it tells the web server what network interface to listen to for connections from clients. By default, Flask's development web server listens for connections on localhost, so only connections originating from within the computer running the server are accepted. The following command makes the web server listen for connections on the public network interface, enabling other computers in the network to connect as well:

```
(venv) $ python hello.py runserver --host 0.0.0.0
 * Running on http://0.0.0.0:5000/
 * Restarting with reloader
```

The web server should now be accessible from any computer in the network at *http://a.b.c.d:5000*, where "a.b.c.d" is the external IP address of the computer running the server.

This chapter introduced the concept of responses to requests, but there is a lot more to say about responses. Flask provides very good support for generating responses using *templates*, and this is such an important topic that the next chapter is dedicated to it.

CHAPTER 3
Templates

The key to writing applications that are easy to maintain is to write clean and well-structured code. The examples that you have seen so far are too simple to demonstrate this, but Flask view functions have two completely independent purposes disguised as one, which creates a problem.

The obvious task of a view function is to generate a response to a request, as you have seen in the examples shown in Chapter 2. For the simplest requests this is enough, but in general a request triggers a change in the state of the application, and the view function is also where this change is generated.

For example, consider a user who is registering a new account on a website. The user types an email address and a password in a web form and clicks the Submit button. On the server, a request that includes the data from the user arrives and Flask dispatches it to the view function that handles registration requests. This view function needs to talk to the database to get the new user added and then generate a response to send back to the browser. These two types of tasks are formally called *business logic* and *presentation logic*, respectively.

Mixing business and presentation logic leads to code that is hard to understand and maintain. Imagine having to build the HTML code for a large table by concatenating data obtained from the database with the necessary HTML string literals. Moving the presentation logic into *templates* helps improve the maintainability of the application.

A template is a file that contains the text of a response, with placeholder variables for the dynamic parts that will be known only in the context of a request. The process that replaces the variables with actual values and returns a final response string is called *rendering*. For the task of rendering templates, Flask uses a powerful template engine called *Jinja2*.

The Jinja2 Template Engine

In its simplest form, a Jinja2 template is a file that contains the text of a response. Example 3-1 shows a Jinja2 template that matches the response of the index() view function of Example 2-1.

Example 3-1. templates/index.html: Jinja2 template

```
<h1>Hello World!</h1>
```

The response returned by view function user() of Example 2-2 has a dynamic component, which is represented by a *variable*. Example 3-2 shows the template that implements this response.

Example 3-2. templates/user.html: Jinja2 template

```
<h1>Hello, {{ name }}!</h1>
```

Rendering Templates

By default Flask looks for templates in a *templates* subfolder located inside the application folder. For the next version of *hello.py*, you need to store the templates defined earlier in a new *templates* folder as *index.html* and *user.html*.

The view functions in the application need to be modified to render these templates. Example 3-3 shows these changes.

Example 3-3. hello.py: Rendering a template

```
from flask import Flask, render_template

# ...

@app.route('/index')
def index():
    return render_template('index.html')

@app.route('/user/<name>')
def user(name):
    return render_template('user.html', name=name)
```

The function render_template provided by Flask integrates the Jinja2 template engine with the application. This function takes the filename of the template as its first argument. Any additional arguments are key/value pairs that represent actual values for variables referenced in the template. In this example, the second template is receiving a name variable.

Keyword arguments like name=name in the previous example are fairly common but may seem confusing and hard to understand if you are not used to them. The "name" on the left side represents the argument name, which is used in the placeholder written in the template. The "name" on the right side is a variable in the current scope that provides the value for the argument of the same name.

 If you have cloned the application's Git repository on GitHub, you can run git checkout 3a to check out this version of the application.

Variables

The {{ name }} construct used in the template shown in Example 3-2 references a variable, a special placeholder that tells the template engine that the value that goes in that place should be obtained from data provided at the time the template is rendered.

Jinja2 recognizes variables of any type, even complex types such as lists, dictionaries and objects. The following are some more examples of variables used in templates:

```
<p>A value from a dictionary: {{ mydict['key'] }}.</p>
<p>A value from a list: {{ mylist[3] }}.</p>
<p>A value from a list, with a variable index: {{ mylist[myintvar] }}.</p>
<p>A value from an object's method: {{ myobj.somemethod() }}.</p>
```

Variables can be modified with *filters*, which are added after the variable name with a pipe character as separator. For example, the following template shows the name variable capitalized:

```
Hello, {{ name|capitalize }}
```

Table 3-1 lists some of the commonly used filters that come with Jinja2.

Table 3-1. Jinja2 variable filters

Filter name	Description
safe	Renders the value without applying escaping
capitalize	Converts the first character of the value to uppercase and the rest to lowercase
lower	Converts the value to lowercase characters
upper	Converts the value to uppercase characters
title	Capitalizes each word in the value
trim	Removes leading and trailing whitespace from the value
striptags	Removes any HTML tags from the value before rendering

The safe filter is interesting to highlight. By default Jinja2 *escapes* all variables for security purposes. For example, if a variable is set to the value '<h1>Hello</h1>', Jinja2 will render the string as `'&lt;h1&gt;Hello&lt;/h1&gt;'`, which will cause the h1 element to be displayed and not interpreted by the browser. Many times it is necessary to display HTML code stored in variables, and for those cases the `safe` filter is used.

 Never use the `safe` filter on values that aren't trusted, such as text entered by users on web forms.

The complete list of filters can be obtained from the official Jinja2 documentation (*http://bit.ly/jinja-filters*).

Control Structures

Jinja2 offers several control structures that can be used to alter the flow of the template. This section introduces some of the most useful ones with simple examples.

The following example shows how conditional statements can be entered in a template:

```
{% if user %}
    Hello, {{ user }}!
{% else %}
    Hello, Stranger!
{% endif %}
```

Another common need in templates is to render a list of elements. This example shows how this can be done with a `for` loop:

```
<ul>
    {% for comment in comments %}
        <li>{{ comment }}</li>
    {% endfor %}
</ul>
```

Jinja2 also supports *macros*, which are similar to functions in Python code. For example:

```
{% macro render_comment(comment) %}
    <li>{{ comment }}</li>
{% endmacro %}

<ul>
    {% for comment in comments %}
        {{ render_comment(comment) }}
    {% endfor %}
</ul>
```

To make macros more reusable, they can be stored in standalone files that are then *imported* from all the templates that need them:

```
{% import 'macros.html' as macros %}
<ul>
    {% for comment in comments %}
        {{ macros.render_comment(comment) }}
    {% endfor %}
</ul>
```

Portions of template code that need to be repeated in several places can be stored in a separate file and *included* from all the templates to avoid repetition:

```
{% include 'common.html' %}
```

Yet another powerful way to reuse is through template inheritance, which is similar to class inheritance in Python code. First, a base template is created with the name *base.html*:

```
<html>
<head>
    {% block head %}
    <title>{% block title %}{% endblock %} - My Application</title>
    {% endblock %}
</head>
<body>
    {% block body %}
    {% endblock %}
</body>
</html>
```

Here the block tags define elements that a derived template can change. In this example, there are blocks called head, title, and body; note that title is contained by head. The following example is a derived template of the base template:

```
{% extends "base.html" %}
{% block title %}Index{% endblock %}
{% block head %}
    {{ super() }}
    <style>
    </style>
{% endblock %}
{% block body %}
<h1>Hello, World!</h1>
{% endblock %}
```

The extends directive declares that this template derives from *base.html*. This directive is followed by new definitions for the three blocks defined in the base template, which are inserted in the proper places. Note that the new definition of the head block, which is not empty in the base template, uses super() to retain the original contents.

Real-world usage of all the control structures presented in this section will be shown later, so you will have the opportunity to see how they work.

Twitter Bootstrap Integration with Flask-Bootstrap

Bootstrap (*http://getbootstrap.com*) is an open source framework from Twitter that provides user interface components to create clean and attractive web pages that are compatible with all modern web browsers.

Bootstrap is a client-side framework, so the server is not directly involved with it. All the server needs to do is provide HTML responses that reference Bootstrap's cascading style sheets (CSS) and JavaScript files and instantiate the desired components through HTML, CSS, and JavaScript code. The ideal place to do all this is in templates.

The obvious way to integrate Bootstrap with the application is to make all the necessary changes to the templates. A simpler approach is to use a Flask *extension* called Flask-Bootstrap to simplify the integration effort. Flask-Bootstrap can be installed with pip:

```
(venv) $ pip install flask-bootstrap
```

Flask extensions are usually initialized at the same time the application instance is created. Example 3-4 shows the initialization of Flask-Bootstrap.

Example 3-4. hello.py: Flask-Bootstrap initialization

```
from flask.ext.bootstrap import Bootstrap
# ...
bootstrap = Bootstrap(app)
```

Like Flask-Script in Chapter 2, Flask-Bootstrap is imported from the `flask.ext` namespace and initialized by passing the application instance in the constructor.

Once Flask-Bootstrap is initialized, a base template that includes all the Bootstrap files is available to the application. This template takes advantage of Jinja2's template inheritance; the application extends a base template that has the general structure of the page including the elements that import Bootstrap. Example 3-5 shows a new version of *user.html* as a derived template.

Example 3-5. templates/user.html: Template that uses Flask-Bootstrap

```
{% extends "bootstrap/base.html" %}

{% block title %}Flasky{% endblock %}

{% block navbar %}
<div class="navbar navbar-inverse" role="navigation">
    <div class="container">
        <div class="navbar-header">
            <button type="button" class="navbar-toggle"
              data-toggle="collapse" data-target=".navbar-collapse">
                <span class="sr-only">Toggle navigation</span>
                <span class="icon-bar"></span>
                <span class="icon-bar"></span>
                <span class="icon-bar"></span>
```

```
            </button>
            <a class="navbar-brand" href="/">Flasky</a>
        </div>
        <div class="navbar-collapse collapse">
            <ul class="nav navbar-nav">
                <li><a href="/">Home</a></li>
            </ul>
        </div>
    </div>
</div>
{% endblock %}

{% block content %}
<div class="container">
    <div class="page-header">
        <h1>Hello, {{ name }}!</h1>
    </div>
</div>
{% endblock %}
```

The Jinja2 extends directive implements the template inheritance by referencing *bootstrap/base.html* from Flask-Bootstrap. The base template from Flask-Bootstrap provides a skeleton web page that includes all the Bootstrap CSS and JavaScript files.

Base templates define *blocks* that can be overriden by derived templates. The block and endblock directives define blocks of content that are added to the base template.

The *user.html* template above defines three blocks called title, navbar, and content. These are all blocks that the base template exports for derived templates to define. The title block is straightforward; its contents will appear between <title> tags in the header of the rendered HTML document. The navbar and content blocks are reserved for the page navigation bar and main content.

In this template, the navbar block defines a simple navigation bar using Bootstrap components. The content block has a container <div> with a page header inside. The greeting line that was in the previous version of the template is now inside the page header. Figure 3-1 shows how the application looks with these changes.

If you have cloned the application's Git repository on GitHub, you can run git checkout 3b to check out this version of the application. The Bootstrap official documentation (*http://getbootstrap.com/*) is a great learning resource full of copy/paste-ready examples.

Figure 3-1. Twitter Bootstrap templates

Flask-Bootstrap's *base.html* template defines several other blocks that can be used in derived templates. Table 3-2 shows the complete list of available blocks.

Table 3-2. Flask-Bootstrap's base template blocks

Block name	Description
doc	The entire HTML document
html_attribs	Attributes inside the <html> tag
html	The contents of the <html> tag
head	The contents of the <head> tag
title	The contents of the <title> tag
metas	The list of <meta> tags
styles	Cascading stylesheet definitions
body_attribs	Attributes inside the <body> tag
body	The contents of the <body> tag
navbar	User-defined navigation bar
content	User-defined page content
scripts	JavaScript declarations at the bottom of the document

Many of the blocks in Table 3-2 are used by Flask-Bootstrap itself, so overriding them directly would cause problems. For example, the styles and scripts blocks are where the Bootstrap files are declared. If the application needs to add its own content to a block that already has some content, then Jinja2's super() function must be used. For example, this is how the `scripts` block would need to be written in the derived template to add a new JavaScript file to the document:

```
{% block scripts %}
{{ super() }}
<script type="text/javascript" src="my-script.js"></script>
{% endblock %}
```

Custom Error Pages

When you enter an invalid route in your browser's address bar, you get a code 404 error page. The error page is now too plain and unattractive, and it has no consistency with the page that uses Bootstrap.

Flask allows an application to define custom error pages that can be based on templates, like regular routes. The two most common error codes are 404, triggered when the client requests a page or route that is not known, and 500, triggered when there is an unhandled exception. Example 3-6 shows how to provide custom handlers for these two errors.

Example 3-6. hello.py: Custom error pages

```
@app.errorhandler(404)
def page_not_found(e):
    return render_template('404.html'), 404

@app.errorhandler(500)
def internal_server_error(e):
    return render_template('500.html'), 500
```

Error handlers return a response, like view functions. They also return the numeric status code that corresponds to the error.

The templates referenced in the error handlers need to be written. These templates should follow the same layout of the regular pages, so in this case they will have a navigation bar and a page header that shows the error message.

The straightforward way to write these templates is to copy *templates/user.html* to *templates/404.html* and *templates/500.html* and then change the page header element in these two new files to the appropriate error message, but this will generate a lot of duplication.

Jinja2's template inheritance can help with this. In the same way Flask-Bootstrap provides a base template with the basic layout of the page, the application can define its own base template with a more complete page layout that includes the navigation bar and leaves the page content to be defined in derived templates. Example 3-7 shows *templates/base.html*, a new template that inherits from *bootstrap/base.html* and defines the navigation bar, but is itself a base template to other templates such as *templates/user.html*, *templates/404.html*, and *templates/500.html*.

Example 3-7. templates/base.html: Base application template with navigation bar

```
{% extends "bootstrap/base.html" %}

{% block title %}Flasky{% endblock %}

{% block navbar %}
<div class="navbar navbar-inverse" role="navigation">
    <div class="container">
        <div class="navbar-header">
            <button type="button" class="navbar-toggle"
              data-toggle="collapse" data-target=".navbar-collapse">
                <span class="sr-only">Toggle navigation</span>
                <span class="icon-bar"></span>
                <span class="icon-bar"></span>
                <span class="icon-bar"></span>
            </button>
            <a class="navbar-brand" href="/">Flasky</a>
        </div>
        <div class="navbar-collapse collapse">
            <ul class="nav navbar-nav">
                <li><a href="/">Home</a></li>
            </ul>
        </div>
    </div>
</div>
{% endblock %}

{% block content %}
<div class="container">
    {% block page_content %}{% endblock %}
</div>
{% endblock %}
```

In the content block of this template is just a container `<div>` element that wraps a new empty block called `page_content`, which derived templates can define.

The templates of the application will now inherit from this template instead of directly from Flask-Bootstrap. Example 3-8 shows how simple it is to construct a custom code 404 error page that inherits from *templates/base.html*.

Example 3-8. templates/404.html: Custom code 404 error page using template inheritance

```
{% extends "base.html" %}

{% block title %}Flasky - Page Not Found{% endblock %}

{% block page_content %}
<div class="page-header">
    <h1>Not Found</h1>
```

```
</div>
{% endblock %}
```

Figure 3-2 shows how the error page looks in the browser.

Figure 3-2. Custom code 404 error page

The *templates/user.html* template can now be simplified by making it inherit from the base template, as shown in Example 3-9.

Example 3-9. templates/user.html: Simplified page template using template inheritance

```
{% extends "base.html" %}

{% block title %}Flasky{% endblock %}

{% block page_content %}
<div class="page-header">
    <h1>Hello, {{ name }}!</h1>
</div>
{% endblock %}
```

 If you have cloned the application's Git repository on GitHub, you can run `git checkout 3c` to check out this version of the application.

Links

Any application that has more than one route will invariably need to include links that connect the different pages, such as in a navigation bar.

Writing the URLs as links directly in the template is trivial for simple routes, but for dynamic routes with variable portions it can get more complicated to build the URLs right in the template. Also, URLs written explicitly create an unwanted dependency on the routes defined in the code. If the routes are reorganized, links in templates may break.

To avoid these problems, Flask provides the url_for() helper function, which generates URLs from the information stored in the application's URL map.

In its simplest usage, this function takes the view function name (or *endpoint* name for routes defined with app.add_url_route()) as its single argument and returns its URL. For example, in the current version of *hello.py* the call url_for('index') would return /. Calling url_for('index', _external=True) would instead return an absolute URL, which in this example is *http://localhost:5000/*.

 Relative URLs are sufficient when generating links that connect the different routes of the application. Absolute URLs are necessary only for links that will be used outside of the web browser, such as when sending links by email.

Dynamic URLs can be generated with url_for() by passing the dynamic parts as keyword arguments. For example, url_for('user', name='john', _external=True) would return *http://localhost:5000/user/john*.

The keyword arguments sent to url_for() are not limited to arguments used by dynamic routes. The function will add any extra arguments to the query string. For example, url_for('index', page=2) would return */?page=2*.

Static Files

Web applications are not made of Python code and templates alone. Most applications also use static files such as images, JavaScript source files, and CSS that are referenced from the HTML code.

You may recall that when the *hello.py* application's URL map was inspected in Chapter 2, a static entry appeared in it. This is so because references to static files are treated as a special route defined as */static/<filename>*. For example, a call to url_for('static', filename='css/styles.css', _external=True) would return *http://localhost:5000/static/css/styles.css*.

In its default configuration, Flask looks for static files in a subdirectory called *static* located in the application's root folder. Files can be organized in subdirectories inside this folder if desired. When the server receives the URL from the previous example, it generates a response that includes the contents of a file in the filesystem located at *static/css/styles.css*.

Example 3-10 shows how the application can include a *favicon.ico* icon in the base template for browsers to show in the address bar.

Example 3-10. templates/base.html: favicon definition

```
{% block head %}
{{ super() }}
<link rel="shortcut icon" href="{{ url_for('static', filename = 'favicon.ico') }}"
    type="image/x-icon">
<link rel="icon" href="{{ url_for('static', filename = 'favicon.ico') }}"
    type="image/x-icon">
{% endblock %}
```

The icon declaration is inserted at the end of the head block. Note how super() is used to preserve the original contents of the block defined in the base templates.

If you have cloned the application's Git repository on GitHub, you can run git checkout 3d to check out this version of the application.

Localization of Dates and Times with Flask-Moment

Handling of dates and times in a web application is not a trivial problem when users work in different parts of the world.

The server needs uniform time units that are independent of the location of each user, so typically Coordinated Universal Time (UTC) is used. For users, however, seeing times expressed in UTC can be confusing, as users always expect to see dates and times presented in their local time and formatted according to the local customs of their region.

An elegant solution that allows the server to work exclusively in UTC is to send these time units to the web browser, where they are converted to local time and rendered. Web browsers can do a much better job at this task because they have access to time zone and locale settings on the user's computer.

There is an excellent client-side open source library written in JavaScript that renders dates and times in the browser called moment.js (*http://momentjs.com*). Flask-Moment is an extension for Flask applications that integrates *moment.js* into Jinja2 templates. Flask-Moment is installed with pip:

```
(venv) $ pip install flask-moment
```

The extension is initialized as shown in Example 3-11.

Example 3-11. hello.py: Initialize Flask-Moment

```
from flask.ext.moment import Moment
moment = Moment(app)
```

Flask-Moment depends on *jquery.js* in addition to *moment.js*. These two libraries need to be included somewhere in the HTML document—either directly, in which case you can choose what versions to use, or through the helper functions provided by the extension, which reference tested versions of these libraries from a Content Delivery Network (CDN). Because Bootstrap already includes *jquery.js*, only *moment.js* needs to be added in this case. Example 3-12 shows how this library is loaded in the scripts of the base template.

Example 3-12. templates/base.html: Import moment.js library

```
{% block scripts %}
{{ super() }}
{{ moment.include_moment() }}
{% endblock %}
```

To work with timestamps Flask-Moment makes a moment class available to templates. The example in Example 3-13 passes a variable called current_time to the template for rendering.

Example 3-13. hello.py: Add a datetime variable

```
from datetime import datetime

@app.route('/')
def index():
    return render_template('index.html',
                           current_time=datetime.utcnow())
```

Example 3-14 shows how current_time is rendered in the template.

Example 3-14. templates/index.html: Timestamp rendering with Flask-Moment

```
<p>The local date and time is {{ moment(current_time).format('LLL') }}.</p>
<p>That was {{ moment(current_time).fromNow(refresh=True) }}</p>
```

The format('LLL') format renders the date and time according to the time zone and locale settings in the client computer. The argument determines the rendering style, from 'L' to 'LLLL' for different levels of verbosity. The format() function can also accept custom format specifiers.

The fromNow() render style shown in the second line renders a relative timestamp and automatically refreshes it as time passes. Initially this timestamp will be shown as "a few seconds ago," but the refresh option will keep it updated as time passes, so if you leave the page open for a few minutes you will see the text changing to "a minute ago," then "2 minutes ago," and so on.

If you have cloned the application's Git repository on GitHub, you can run `git checkout 3e` to check out this version of the application.

Flask-Moment implements the `format()`, `fromNow()`, `fromTime()`, `calendar()`, `valueOf()`, and `unix()` methods from *moment.js*. Consult the documentation (*http://momentjs.com/docs/#/displaying/*) to learn about all the formatting options offered.

Flask-Moment assumes that timestamps handled by the server-side application are "naive" `datetime` objects expressed in UTC. See the documentation for the `datetime` (*http://bit.ly/datepack*) package in the standard library for information on naive and aware date and time objects.

The timestamps rendered by Flask-Moment can be localized to many languages. A language can be selected in the template by passing the language code to function `lang()`:

```
{{ moment.lang('es') }}
```

With all the techniques discussed in this chapter, you should be able to build modern and user-friendly web pages for your application. The next chapter touches on an aspect of templates not yet discussed: how to interact with the user through web forms.

## CHAPTER 4

Web Forms

The request object, introduced in Chapter 2, exposes all the information sent by the client with a request. In particular, `request.form` provides access to form data submitted in POST requests.

Although the support provided in Flask's request object is sufficient for the handling of web forms, there are a number of tasks that can become tedious and repetitive. Two good examples are the generation of HTML code for forms and the validation of the submitted form data.

The Flask-WTF (*http://pythonhosted.org/Flask-WTF/*) extension makes working with web forms a much more pleasant experience. This extension is a Flask integration wrapper around the framework-agnostic WTForms (*http://wtforms.simpleco des.com/*) package.

Flask-WTF and its dependencies can be installed with `pip`:

```
(venv) $ pip install flask-wtf
```

Cross-Site Request Forgery (CSRF) Protection

By default, Flask-WTF protects all forms against Cross-Site Request Forgery (CSRF) attacks. A CSRF attack occurs when a malicious website sends requests to a different website on which the victim is logged in.

To implement CSRF protection, Flask-WTF needs the application to configure an encryption key. Flask-WTF uses this key to generate encrypted tokens that are used to verify the authenticity of requests with form data. Example 4-1 shows how to configure an encryption key.

Example 4-1. hello.py: Flask-WTF configuration

```
app = Flask(__name__)
app.config['SECRET_KEY'] = 'hard to guess string'
```

The `app.config` dictionary is a general-purpose place to store configuration variables used by the framework, the extensions, or the application itself. Configuration values can be added to the `app.config` object using standard dictionary syntax. The configuration object also has methods to import configuration values from files or the environment.

The `SECRET_KEY` configuration variable is used as a general-purpose encryption key by Flask and several third-party extensions. As its name implies, the strength of the encryption depends on the value of this variable being secret. Pick a different secret key in each application that you build and make sure that this string is not known by anyone.

 For added security, the secret key should be stored in an environment variable instead of being embedded in the code. This technique is described in Chapter 7.

Form Classes

When using Flask-WTF, each web form is represented by a class that inherits from class `Form`. The class defines the list of fields in the form, each represented by an object. Each field object can have one or more *validators* attached; validators are functions that check whether the input submitted by the user is valid.

Example 4-2 shows a simple web form that has a text field and a submit button.

Example 4-2. hello.py: Form class definition

```
from flask.ext.wtf import Form
from wtforms import StringField, SubmitField
from wtforms.validators import Required

class NameForm(Form):
    name = StringField('What is your name?', validators=[Required()])
    submit = SubmitField('Submit')
```

The fields in the form are defined as class variables, and each class variable is assigned an object associated with the field type. In the previous example, the `NameForm` form has a text field called `name` and a submit button called `submit`. The `StringField` class represents an `<input>` element with a `type="text"` attribute. The `SubmitField` class represents an `<input>` element with a `type="submit"` attribute. The first argument to the field constructors is the label that will be used when rendering the form to HTML.

The optional `validators` argument included in the `StringField` constructor defines a list of checkers that will be applied to the data submitted by the user before it is accepted. The `Required()` validator ensures that the field is not submitted empty.

 The `Form` base class is defined by the Flask-WTF extension, so it is imported from `flask.ext.wtf`. The fields and validators, however, are imported directly from the WTForms package.

The list of standard HTML fields supported by WTForms is shown in Table 4-1.

Table 4-1. WTForms standard HTML fields

Field type	Description
StringField	Text field
TextAreaField	Multiple-line text field
PasswordField	Password text field
HiddenField	Hidden text field
DateField	Text field that accepts a `datetime.date` value in a given format
DateTimeField	Text field that accepts a `datetime.datetime` value in a given format
IntegerField	Text field that accepts an integer value
DecimalField	Text field that accepts a `decimal.Decimal` value
FloatField	Text field that accepts a floating-point value
BooleanField	Checkbox with `True` and `False` values
RadioField	List of radio buttons
SelectField	Drop-down list of choices
SelectMultipleField	Drop-down list of choices with multiple selection
FileField	File upload field
SubmitField	Form submission button
FormField	Embed a form as a field in a container form
FieldList	List of fields of a given type

The list of WTForms built-in validators is shown in Table 4-2.

Table 4-2. WTForms validators

Validator	Description
Email	Validates an email address
EqualTo	Compares the values of two fields; useful when requesting a password to be entered twice for confirmation
IPAddress	Validates an IPv4 network address
Length	Validates the length of the string entered
NumberRange	Validates that the value entered is within a numeric range
Optional	Allows empty input on the field, skipping additional validators
Required	Validates that the field contains data
Regexp	Validates the input against a regular expression
URL	Validates a URL
AnyOf	Validates that the input is one of a list of possible values
NoneOf	Validates that the input is none of a list of possible values

HTML Rendering of Forms

Form fields are callables that, when invoked, from a template render themselves to HTML. Assuming that the view function passes a NameForm instance to the template as an argument named form, the template can generate a simple HTML form as follows:

```
<form method="POST">
    {{ form.name.label }} {{ form.name() }}
    {{ form.submit() }}
</form>
```

Of course, the result is extremely bare. To improve the look of the form, any arguments sent into the calls that render the fields are converted into HTML attributes for the field; so, for example, you can give the field id or class attributes and then define CSS styles:

```
<form method="POST">
    {{ form.name.label }} {{ form.name(id='my-text-field') }}
    {{ form.submit() }}
</form>
```

But even with HTML attributes, the effort required to render a form in this way is significant, so it is best to leverage Bootstrap's own set of form styles whenever possible. Flask-Bootstrap provides a very high-level helper function that renders an entire Flask-WTF form using Bootstrap's predefined form styles, all with a single call. Using Flask-Bootstrap, the previous form can be rendered as follows:

```
{% import "bootstrap/wtf.html" as wtf %}
{{ wtf.quick_form(form) }}
```

The `import` directive works in the same way as regular Python scripts do and allows template elements to be imported and used in many templates. The imported *bootstrap/wtf.html* file defines helper functions that render Flask-WTF forms using Bootstrap. The `wtf.quick_form()` function takes a Flask-WTF form object and renders it using default Bootstrap styles. The complete template for *hello.py* is shown in Example 4-3.

Example 4-3. templates/index.html: Using Flask-WTF and Flask-Bootstrap to render a form

```
{% extends "base.html" %}
{% import "bootstrap/wtf.html" as wtf %}

{% block title %}Flasky{% endblock %}

{% block page_content %}
<div class="page-header">
    <h1>Hello, {% if name %}{{ name }}{% else %}Stranger{% endif %}!</h1>
</div>
{{ wtf.quick_form(form) }}
{% endblock %}
```

The content area of the template now has two sections. The first section is a page header that shows a greeting. Here a template conditional is used. Conditionals in Jinja2 have the format `{% if variable %}`...`{% else %}`...`{% endif %}`. If the condition evaluates to `True`, then what appears between the `if` and `else` directives is rendered to the template. If the condition evaluates to `False`, then what's between the `else` and `endif` is rendered. The example template will render the string "Hello, Stranger!" when the `name` template argument is undefined. The second section of the content renders the `NameForm` object using the `wtf.quick_form()` function.

Form Handling in View Functions

In the new version of *hello.py*, the `index()` view function will be rendering the form and also receiving its data. Example 4-4 shows the updated `index()` view function.

Example 4-4. hello.py: Route methods

```
@app.route('/', methods=['GET', 'POST'])
def index():
    name = None
    form = NameForm()
    if form.validate_on_submit():
        name = form.name.data
        form.name.data = ''
    return render_template('index.html', form=form, name=name)
```

The methods argument added to the app.route decorator tells Flask to register the view function as a handler for GET and POST requests in the URL map. When methods is not given, the view function is registered to handle GET requests only.

Adding POST to the method list is necessary because form submissions are much more conveniently handled as POST requests. It is possible to submit a form as a GET request, but as GET requests have no body, the data is appended to the URL as a query string and becomes visible in the browser's address bar. For this and several other reasons, form submissions are almost universally done as POST requests.

The local name variable is used to hold the name received from the form when available; when the name is not known the variable is initialized to None. The view function creates an instance of the NameForm class shown previously to represent the form. The validate_on_submit() method of the form returns True when the form was submitted and the data has been accepted by all the field validators. In all other cases, validate_on_submit() returns False. The return value of this method effectively serves to decide whether the form needs to be rendered or processed.

When a user navigates to the application for the first time, the server will receive a GET request with no form data, so validate_on_submit() will return False. The body of the if statement will be skipped and the request will be handled by rendering the template, which gets the form object and the name variable set to None as arguments. Users will now see the form displayed in the browser.

When the form is submitted by the user, the server receives a POST request with the data. The call to validate_on_submit() invokes the Required() validator attached to the name field. If the name is not empty, then the validator accepts it and validate_on_submit() returns True. Now the name entered by the user is accessible as the data attribute of the field. Inside the body of the if statement, this name is assigned to the local name variable and the form field is cleared by setting that data attribute to an empty string. The render_template() call in the last line renders the template, but this time the name argument contains the name from the form, so the greeting will be personalized.

 If you have cloned the application's Git repository on GitHub, you can run git checkout 4a to check out this version of the application.

Figure 4-1 shows how the form looks in the browser window when a user initially enters the site. When the user submits a name, the application responds with a personalized greeting. The form still appears below it, so a user can submit it with a new name if desired. Figure 4-2 shows the application in this state.

Figure 4-1. Flask-WTF web form

If the user submits the form with an empty name, the Required() validatior catches the error, as seen in Figure 4-3. Note how much functionality is being provided automatically. This is a great example of the power that well-designed extensions like Flask-WTF and Flask-Bootstrap can give to your application.

Figure 4-2. Web form after submission

Figure 4-3. Web form after failed validator

Redirects and User Sessions

The last version of *hello.py* has a usability problem. If you enter your name and submit it and then click the refresh button on your browser, you will likely get an obscure warning that asks for confirmation before submitting the form again. This happens because browsers repeat the last request they have sent when they are asked to refresh the page. When the last request sent is a POST request with form data, a refresh would cause a duplicate form submission, which in almost all cases is not the desired action.

Many users do not understand the warning from the browser. For this reason, it is considered good practice for web applications to never leave a POST request as a last request sent by the browser.

This practice can be achieved by responding to POST requests with a *redirect* instead of a normal response. A redirect is a special type of response that has a URL instead of a string with HTML code. When the browser receives this response, it issues a GET request for the redirect URL, and that is the page that is displayed. The page may take a few more milliseconds to load because of the second request that has to be sent to the server, but other than that, the user will not see any difference. Now the last request is a GET, so the refresh command works as expected. This trick is known as the *Post/Redirect/Get pattern*.

But this approach brings a second problem. When the application handles the POST request, it has access to the name entered by the user in form.name.data, but as soon as that request ends the form data is lost. Because the POST request is handled with a redirect, the application needs to store the name so that the redirected request can have it and use it to build the actual response.

Applications can "remember" things from one request to the next by storing them in the *user session*, private storage that is available to each connected client. The user session was introduced in Chapter 2 as one of the variables associated with the request context. It's called session and is accessed like a standard Python dictionary.

 By default, user sessions are stored in client-side cookies that are cryptographically signed using the configured SECRET_KEY. Any tampering with the cookie content would render the signature invalid, thus invalidating the session.

Example 4-5 shows a new version of the index() view function that implements redirects and user sessions.

Example 4-5. hello.py: Redirects and user sessions

```
from flask import Flask, render_template, session, redirect, url_for

@app.route('/', methods=['GET', 'POST'])
def index():
    form = NameForm()
    if form.validate_on_submit():
        session['name'] = form.name.data
        return redirect(url_for('index'))
    return render_template('index.html', form=form, name=session.get('name'))
```

In the previous version of the application, a local name variable was used to store the name entered by the user in the form. That variable is now placed in the user session as session['name'] so that it is remembered beyond the request.

Requests that come with valid form data will now end with a call to redirect(), a helper function that generates the HTTP redirect response. The redirect() function takes the URL to redirect to as an argument. The redirect URL used in this case is the root URL, so the response could have been written more concisely as redirect('/'), but instead Flask's URL generator function url_for() is used. The use of url_for() to generate URLs is encouraged because this function generates URLs using the URL map, so URLs are guaranteed to be compatible with defined routes and any changes made to route names will be automatically available when using this function.

The first and only required argument to url_for() is the *endpoint* name, the internal name each route has. By default, the endpoint of a route is the name of the view function attached to it. In this example, the view function that handles the root URL is index(), so the name given to url_for() is index.

The last change is in the render_template() function, which now obtains the name argument directly from the session using session.get('name'). As with regular dictionaries, using get() to request a dictionary key avoids an exception for keys that aren't found, because get() returns a default value of None for a missing key.

 If you have cloned the application's Git repository on GitHub, you can run git checkout 4b to check out this version of the application.

With this version of the application, you can see that refreshing the page in your browser results in the expected behavior.

Message Flashing

Sometimes it is useful to give the user a status update after a request is completed. This could be a confirmation message, a warning, or an error. A typical example is when you submit a login form to a website with a mistake and the server responds by rendering the login form again with a message above it that informs you that your username or password is invalid.

Flask includes this functionality as a core feature. Example 4-6 shows how the flash() function can be used for this purpose.

Example 4-6. hello.py: Flashed messages

```
from flask import Flask, render_template, session, redirect, url_for, flash

@app.route('/', methods=['GET', 'POST'])
def index():
    form = NameForm()
    if form.validate_on_submit():
        old_name = session.get('name')
        if old_name is not None and old_name != form.name.data:
            flash('Looks like you have changed your name!')
        session['name'] = form.name.data
        form.name.data = ''
        return redirect(url_for('index'))
    return render_template('index.html',
        form = form, name = session.get('name'))
```

In this example, each time a name is submitted it is compared against the name stored in the user session, which would have been put there during a previous submission of the same form. If the two names are different, the flash() function is invoked with a message to be displayed on the next response sent back to the client.

Calling `flash()` is not enough to get messages displayed; the templates used by the application need to render these messages. The best place to render flashed messages is the base template, because that will enable these messages in all pages. Flask makes a `get_flashed_messages()` function available to templates to retrieve the messages and render them, as shown in Example 4-7.

Example 4-7. templates/base.html: Flash message rendering

```
{% block content %}
<div class="container">
    {% for message in get_flashed_messages() %}
    <div class="alert alert-warning">
        <button type="button" class="close" data-dismiss="alert">&times;</button>
        {{ message }}
    </div>
    {% endfor %}

    {% block page_content %}{% endblock %}
</div>
{% endblock %}
```

In this example, messages are rendered using Bootstrap's alert CSS styles for warning messages (one is shown in Figure 4-4).

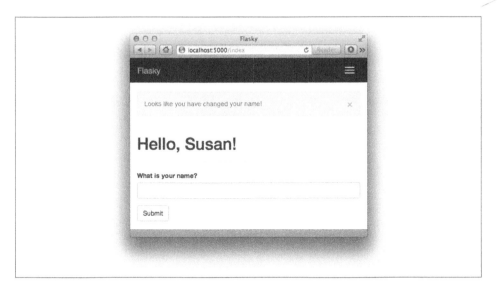

Figure 4-4. Flashed message

A loop is used because there could be multiple messages queued for display, one for each time `flash()` was called in the previous request cycle. Messages that are retrieved from `get_flashed_messages()` will not be returned the next time this function is called, so flashed messages appear only once and are then discarded.

 If you have cloned the application's Git repository on GitHub, you can run `git checkout 4c` to check out this version of the application.

Being able to accept data from the user through web forms is a feature required by most applications, and so is the ability to store that data in permanent storage. Using databases with Flask is the topic of the next chapter.

## CHAPTER 5

Databases

A *database* stores application data in an organized way. The application then issues *queries* to retrieve specific portions as they are needed. The most commonly used databases for web applications are those based on the *relational* model, also called SQL databases in reference to the Structured Query Language they use. But in recent years *document-oriented* and *key-value* databases, informally known together as NoSQL databases, have become popular alternatives.

SQL Databases

Relational databases store data in *tables*, which model the different entities in the application's domain. For example, a database for an order management application will likely have `customers`, `products`, and `orders` tables.

A table has a fixed number of *columns* and a variable number of *rows*. The columns define the data attributes of the entity represented by the table. For example, a `customers` table will have columns such as `name`, `address`, `phone`, and so on. Each row in a table defines an actual data element that consists of values for all the columns.

Tables have a special column called the *primary key*, which holds a unique identifier for each row stored in the table. Tables can also have columns called *foreign keys*, which reference the primary key of another row from the same or another table. These links between rows are called *relationships* and are the foundation of the relational database model.

Figure 5-1 shows a diagram of a simple database with two tables that store users and user roles. The line that connects the two tables represents a relationship between the tables.

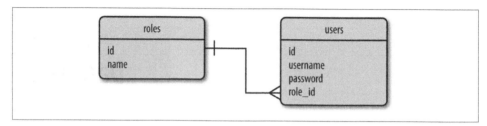

Figure 5-1. Relational database example

In this database diagram, the roles table stores the list of all possible user roles, each identified by a unique id value—the table's primary key. The users table contains the list of users, each with its own unique id as well. Besides the id primary keys, the roles table has a name column and the users table has username and password columns. The role_id column in the users table is a foreign key that references the id of a role, and in this way the role assigned to each user is established.

As seen in the example, relational databases store data efficiently and avoid duplication. Renaming a user role in this database is simple because role names exist in a single place. Immediately after a role name is changed in the roles table, all users that have a role_id that references the changed role will see the update.

On the other hand, having the data split into multiple tables can be a complication. Producing a listing of users with their roles presents a small problem, because users and user roles need to be read from two tables and *joined* before they can be presented together. Relational database engines provide the support to perform join operations between tables when necessary.

NoSQL Databases

Databases that do not follow the relational model described in the previous section are collectively referred to as *NoSQL* databases. One common organization for NoSQL databases uses *collections* instead of tables and *documents* instead of records. NoSQL databases are designed in a way that makes joins difficult, so most of them do not support this operation at all. For a NoSQL database structured as in Figure 5-1, listing the users with their roles requires the application itself to perform the join operation by reading the role_id field of each user and then searching the roles table for it.

A more appropriate design for a NoSQL database is shown in Figure 5-2. This is the result of applying an operation called *denormalization*, which reduces the number of tables at the expense of data duplication.

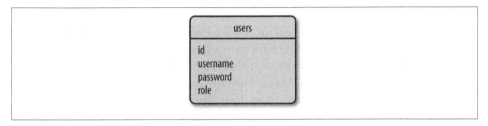

Figure 5-2. NoSQL database example

A database with this structure has the role name explicitly stored with each user. Renaming a role can then turn out to be an expensive operation that may require updating a large number of documents.

But it isn't all bad news with NoSQL databases. Having the data duplicated allows for faster querying. Listing users and their roles is straightforward because no joins are needed.

SQL or NoSQL?

SQL databases excel at storing structured data in an efficient and compact form. These databases go to great lengths to preserve consistency. NoSQL databases relax some of the consistency requirements and as a result can sometimes get a performance edge.

A full analysis and comparison of database types is outside the scope of this book. For small- to medium-size applications, both SQL and NoSQL databases are perfectly capable and have practically equivalent performance.

Python Database Frameworks

Python has packages for most database engines, both open source and commercial. Flask puts no restrictions on what database packages can be used, so you can work with MySQL, Postgres, SQLite, Redis, MongoDB, or CouchDB if any of these is your favorite.

As if those weren't enough choices, there are also a number of database abstraction layer packages such as SQLAlchemy or MongoEngine that allow you to work at a higher level with regular Python objects instead of database entities such as tables, documents, or query languages.

There are a number of factors to evaluate when choosing a database framework:

Ease of use
> When comparing straight database engines versus database abstraction layers, the second group clearly wins. Abstraction layers, also called object-relational mappers (ORMs) or object-document mappers (ODMs), provide transparent conversion of high-level object-oriented operations into low-level database instructions.

Performance

> The conversions that ORMs and ODMs have to do to translate from the object domain into the database domain have an overhead. In most cases, the performance penalty is negligible, but they may not always be. In general, the productivity gain obtained with ORMs and ODMs far outweighs a minimal performance degradation, so this isn't a valid argument to drop ORMs and ODMs completely. What makes sense is to choose a database abstraction layer that provides optional access to the underlying database in case specific operations need to be optimized by implementing them directly as native database instructions.

Portability

> The database choices available on your development and production platforms must be considered. For example, if you plan to host your application on a cloud platform, then you should find out what database choices this service offers.

> Another portability aspect applies to ORMs and ODMs. Although some of these frameworks provide an abstraction layer for a single database engine, others abstract even higher and provide a choice of database engines—all accessible with the same object-oriented interface. The best example of this is the SQLAlchemy ORM, which supports a list of relational database engines including the popular MySQL, Postgres, and SQLite.

Flask integration

> Choosing a framework that has integration with Flask is not absolutely required, but it will save you from having to write the integration code yourself. Flask integration could simplify configuration and operation, so using a package specifically designed as a Flask extension should be preferred.

Based on these goals, the chosen database framework for the examples in this book will be Flask-SQLAlchemy (*http://pythonhosted.org/Flask-SQLAlchemy/*), the Flask extension wrapper for SQLAlchemy (*http://www.sqlalchemy.org/*).

Database Management with Flask-SQLAlchemy

Flask-SQLAlchemy is a Flask extension that simplifies the use of SQLAlchemy inside Flask applications. SQLAlchemy is a powerful relational database framework that supports several database backends. It offers a high-level ORM and low level access to the database's native SQL functionality.

Like most other extensions, Flask-SQLAlchemy is installed with pip:

```
(venv) $ pip install flask-sqlalchemy
```

In Flask-SQLAlchemy, a database is specified as a URL. Table 5-1 lists the format of database URLs for the three most popular database engines.

Table 5-1. Flask-SQLAlchemy database URLs

Database engine	URL
MySQL	*mysql://username:password@hostname/database*
Postgres	*postgresql://username:password@hostname/database*
SQLite (Unix)	*sqlite:////absolute/path/to/database*
SQLite (Windows)	*sqlite:///c:/absolute/path/to/database*

In these URLs, *hostname* refers to the server that hosts the MySQL service, which could be *localhost* or a remote server. Database servers can host several databases, so *database* indicates the name of the database to use. For databases that need authentication, *username* and *password* are the database user credentials.

 SQLite databases do not have a server, so *hostname*, *username*, and *password* are omitted and *database* is the filename of a disk file.

The URL of the application database must be configured as the key SQLALCHEMY_DATABASE_URI in the Flask configuration object. Another useful option is the configuration key SQLALCHEMY_COMMIT_ON_TEARDOWN, which can be set to True to enable automatic commits of database changes at the end of each request. Consult the Flask-SQLAlchemy documentation for information on other configuration options. Example 5-1 shows how to initialize and configure a simple SQLite database.

Example 5-1. hello.py: Database configuration

```
from flask.ext.sqlalchemy import SQLAlchemy

basedir = os.path.abspath(os.path.dirname(__file__))

app = Flask(__name__)
app.config['SQLALCHEMY_DATABASE_URI'] =\
    'sqlite:///' + os.path.join(basedir, 'data.sqlite')
app.config['SQLALCHEMY_COMMIT_ON_TEARDOWN'] = True

db = SQLAlchemy(app)
```

The db object instantiated from class SQLAlchemy represents the database and provides access to all the functionality of Flask-SQLAlchemy.

Model Definition

The term *model* is used to refer to the persistent entities used by the application. In the context of an ORM, a model is typically a Python class with attributes that match the columns of a corresponding database table.

The database instance from Flask-SQLAlchemy provides a base class for models as well as a set of helper classes and functions that are used to define their structure. The `roles` and `users` tables from Figure 5-1 can be defined as models `Role` and `User` as shown in Example 5-2.

Example 5-2. hello.py: Role and User model definition

```python
class Role(db.Model):
    __tablename__ = 'roles'
    id = db.Column(db.Integer, primary_key=True)
    name = db.Column(db.String(64), unique=True)

    def __repr__(self):
        return '<Role %r>' % self.name

class User(db.Model):
    __tablename__ = 'users'
    id = db.Column(db.Integer, primary_key=True)
    username = db.Column(db.String(64), unique=True, index=True)

    def __repr__(self):
        return '<User %r>' % self.username
```

The `__tablename__` class variable defines the name of the table in the database. Flask-SQLAlchemy assigns a default table name if `__tablename__` is omitted, but those default names do not follow the convention of using plurals for table names, so it is best to name tables explicitly. The remaining class variables are the attributes of the model, defined as instances of the `db.Column` class.

The first argument given to the `db.Column` constructor is the type of the database column and model attribute. Table 5-2 lists some of the column types that are available, along with the Python type used in the model.

Table 5-2. Most common SQLAlchemy column types

Type name	Python type	Description
Integer	`int`	Regular integer, typically 32 bits
SmallInteger	`int`	Short-range integer, typically 16 bits
BigInteger	`int` or `long`	Unlimited precision integer
Float	`float`	Floating-point number
Numeric	`decimal.Decimal`	Fixed-point number

Type name	Python type	Description
String	`str`	Variable-length string
Text	`str`	Variable-length string, optimized for large or unbound length
Unicode	`unicode`	Variable-length Unicode string
UnicodeText	`unicode`	Variable-length Unicode string, optimized for large or unbound length
Boolean	`bool`	Boolean value
Date	`datetime.date`	Date value
Time	`datetime.time`	Time value
DateTime	`datetime.datetime`	Date and time value
Interval	`datetime.timedelta`	Time interval
Enum	`str`	List of string values
PickleType	Any Python object	Automatic Pickle serialization
LargeBinary	`str`	Binary blob

The remaining arguments to `db.Column` specify configuration options for each attribute. Table 5-3 lists some of the options available.

Table 5-3. Most common SQLAlchemy column options

Option name	Description
`primary_key`	If set to `True`, the column is the table's primary key.
`unique`	If set to `True`, do not allow duplicate values for this column.
`index`	If set to `True`, create an index for this column, so that queries are more efficient.
`nullable`	If set to `True`, allow empty values for this column. If set to `False`, the column will not allow null values.
`default`	Define a default value for the column.

Flask-SQLAlchemy requires all models to define a *primary key* column, which is normally named `id`.

Although it's not strictly necessary, the two models include a `__repr__()` method to give them a readable string representation that can be used for debugging and testing purposes.

Relationships

Relational databases establish connections between rows in different tables through the use of relationships. The relational diagram in Figure 5-1 expresses a simple relationship between users and their roles. This is a *one-to-many* relationship from roles to users, because one role belongs to many users and users have only one role.

Example 5-3 shows how the one-to-many relationship in Figure 5-1 is represented in the model classes.

Example 5-3. hello.py: Relationships

```
class Role(db.Model):
    # ...
    users = db.relationship('User', backref='role')

class User(db.Model):
    # ...
    role_id = db.Column(db.Integer, db.ForeignKey('roles.id'))
```

As seen in Figure 5-1, a relationship connects two rows through the user of a foreign key. The role_id column added to the User model is defined as a foreign key, and that establishes the relationship. The 'roles.id' argument to db.ForeignKey() specifies that the column should be interpreted as having id values from rows in the roles table.

The users attribute added to model Role represents the object-oriented view of the relationship. Given an instance of class Role, the users attribute will return the list of users associated with that role. The first argument to db.relationship() indicates what model is on the other side of the relationship. This model can be provided as a string if the class is not yet defined.

The backref argument to db.relationship() defines the reverse direction of the relationship by adding a role attribute to the User model. This attribute can be used instead of role_id to access the Role model as an object instead of as a foreign key.

In most cases db.relationship() can locate the relationship's foreign key on its own, but sometimes it cannot determine what column to use as a foreign key. For example, if the User model had two or more columns defined as Role foreign keys, then SQLAlchemy would not know which one of the two to use. Whenever the foreign key configuration is ambiguous, additional arguments to db.relationship() need to be given. Table 5-4 lists some of the common configuration options that can be used to define a relationship.

Table 5-4. Common SQLAlchemy relationship options

Option name	Description
backref	Add a back reference in the other model in the relationship.
primaryjoin	Specify the join condition between the two models explicitly. This is necessary only for ambiguous relationships.
lazy	Specify how the related items are to be loaded. Possible values are select (items are loaded on demand the first time they are accessed), immediate (items are loaded when the source object is loaded), joined (items are loaded immediately, but as a join), subquery (items are loaded immediately, but as a subquery), noload (items are never loaded), and dynamic (instead of loading the items the query that can load them is given).
uselist	If set to False, use a scalar instead of a list.
order_by	Specify the ordering used for the items in the relationship.
secondary	Specify the name of the association table to use in *many-to-many* relationships.
secondaryjoin	Specify the secondary join condition for *many-to-many* relationships when SQLAlchemy cannot determine it on its own.

If you have cloned the application's Git repository on GitHub, you can run git checkout 5a to check out this version of the application.

There are other relationship types besides the one-to-many. The *one-to-one* relationship can be expressed as the one-to-many described earlier, but with the uselist option set to False within the db.relationship() definition so that the "many" side becomes a "one" side. The *many-to-one* relationship can also be expressed as a one-to-many if the tables are reversed, or it can be expressed with the foreign key and the db.relationship() definition both on the "many" side. The most complex relationship type, the *many-to-many*, requires an additional table called an *association table*. You will learn about many-to-many relationships in Chapter 12.

Database Operations

The models are now fully configured according to the database diagram in Figure 5-1 and are ready to be used. The best way to learn how to work with these models is in a Python shell. The following sections will walk you through the most common database operations.

Creating the Tables

The very first thing to do is to instruct Flask-SQLAlchemy to create a database based on the model classes. The db.create_all() function does this:

```
(venv) $ python hello.py shell
>>> from hello import db
>>> db.create_all()
```

If you check the application directory, you will now see a new file there called *data.sqlite*, the name that was given to the SQLite database in the configuration. The db.create_all() function will not re-create or update a database table if it already exists in the database. This can be inconvenient when the models are modified and the changes need to be applied to an existing database. The brute-force solution to update existing database tables is to remove the old tables first:

```
>>> db.drop_all()
>>> db.create_all()
```

Unfortunately, this method has the undesired side effect of destroying all the data in the old database. A better solution to the problem of updating databases is presented near the end of the chapter.

Inserting Rows

The following example creates a few roles and users:

```
>>> from hello import Role, User
>>> admin_role = Role(name='Admin')
>>> mod_role = Role(name='Moderator')
>>> user_role = Role(name='User')
>>> user_john = User(username='john', role=admin_role)
>>> user_susan = User(username='susan', role=user_role)
>>> user_david = User(username='david', role=user_role)
```

The constructors for models accept initial values for the model attributes as keyword arguments. Note that even the role attribute can be used, even though it is not a real database column but a high-level representation of the one-to-many relationship. The id attribute of these new objects is not set explicitly: the primary keys are managed by Flask-SQLAlchemy. The objects exist only on the Python side so far; they have not been written to the database yet. Because of that their id value has not yet been assigned:

```
>>> print(admin_role.id)
None
>>> print(mod_role.id)
None
>>> print(user_role.id)
None
```

Changes to the database are managed through a database *session*, which Flask-SQLAlchemy provides as db.session. To prepare objects to be written to the database, they must be added to the session:

```
>>> db.session.add(admin_role)
>>> db.session.add(mod_role)
>>> db.session.add(user_role)
>>> db.session.add(user_john)
>>> db.session.add(user_susan)
>>> db.session.add(user_david)
```

Or, more concisely:

```
>>> db.session.add_all([admin_role, mod_role, user_role,
...      user_john, user_susan, user_david])
```

To write the objects to the database, the session needs to be *committed* by calling its commit() method:

```
>>> db.session.commit()
```

Check the id attributes again; they are now set:

```
>>> print(admin_role.id)
1
>>> print(mod_role.id)
2
>>> print(user_role.id)
3
```

 The db.session database session is not related to the Flask session object discussed in Chapter 4. Database sessions are also called *trans-actions*.

Database sessions are extremely useful in keeping the database consistent. The commit operation writes all the objects that were added to the session atomically. If an error occurs while the session is being written, the whole session is discarded. If you always commit related changes together in a session, you are guaranteed to avoid database inconsistencies due to partial updates.

 A database session can also be *rolled back*. If db.session.rollback() is called, any objects that were added to the database session are restored to the state they have in the database.

Modifying Rows

The add() method of the database session can also be used to update models. Continuing in the same shell session, the following example renames the "Admin" role to "Administrator":

```
>>> admin_role.name = 'Administrator'
>>> db.session.add(admin_role)
>>> db.session.commit()
```

Deleting Rows

The database session also has a delete() method. The following example deletes the "Moderator" role from the database:

```
>>> db.session.delete(mod_role)
>>> db.session.commit()
```

Note that deletions, like insertions and updates, are executed only when the database session is committed.

Querying Rows

Flask-SQLAlchemy makes a query object available in each model class. The most basic query for a model is the one that returns the entire contents of the corresponding table:

```
>>> Role.query.all()
[<Role u'Administrator'>, <Role u'User'>]
>>> User.query.all()
[<User u'john'>, <User u'susan'>, <User u'david'>]
```

A query object can be configured to issue more specific database searches through the use of *filters*. The following example finds all the users that were assigned the "User" role:

```
>>> User.query.filter_by(role=user_role).all()
[<User u'susan'>, <User u'david'>]
```

It is also possible to inspect the native SQL query that SQLAlchemy generates for a given query by converting the query object to a string:

```
>>> str(User.query.filter_by(role=user_role))
'SELECT users.id AS users_id, users.username AS users_username,
users.role_id AS users_role_id FROM users WHERE :param_1 = users.role_id'
```

If you exit the shell session, the objects created in the previous example will cease to exist as Python objects but will continue to exist as rows in their respective database tables. If you then start a brand new shell session, you have to re-create Python objects from their database rows. The following example issues a query that loads the user role with name "User":

```
>>> user_role = Role.query.filter_by(name='User').first()
```

Filters such as `filter_by()` are invoked on a query object and return a new refined query. Multiple filters can be called in sequence until the query is configured as needed.

Table 5-5 shows some of the most common filters available to queries. The complete list is in the SQLAlchemy documentation (*http://docs.sqlalchemy.org*).

Table 5-5. Common SQLAlchemy query filters

Option	Description
filter()	Returns a new query that adds an additional filter to the original query
filter_by()	Returns a new query that adds an additional equality filter to the original query
limit()	Returns a new query that limits the number of results of the original query to the given number
offset()	Returns a new query that applies an offset into the list of results of the original query
order_by()	Returns a new query that sorts the results of the original query according to the given criteria
group_by()	Returns a new query that groups the results of the original query according to the given criteria

After the desired filters have been applied to the query, a call to `all()` will cause the query to execute and return the results as a list, but there are other ways to trigger the execution of a query besides `all()`. Table 5-6 shows other query execution methods.

Table 5-6. Most common SQLAlchemy query executors

Option	Description
all()	Returns all the results of a query as a list
first()	Returns the first result of a query, or None if there are no results
first_or_404()	Returns the first result of a query, or aborts the request and sends a 404 error as response if there are no results
get()	Returns the row that matches the given primary key, or None if no matching row is found
get_or_404()	Returns the row that matches the given primary key. If the key is not found it aborts the request and sends a 404 error as response
count()	Returns the result count of the query
paginate()	Returns a Pagination object that contains the specified range of results

Relationships work similarly to queries. The following example queries the one-to-many relationship between roles and users from both ends:

```
>>> users = user_role.users
>>> users
[<User u'susan'>, <User u'david'>]
>>> users[0].role
<Role u'User'>
```

The `user_role.users` query here has a small problem. The implicit query that runs when the `user_role.users` expression is issued internally calls `all()` to return the list of users. Because the query object is hidden, it is not possible to refine it with additional query filters. In this particular example, it may have been useful to request that the user list be returned in alphabetical order. In Example 5-4, the configuration of the relationship is modified with a `lazy = 'dynamic'` argument to request that the query is not automatically executed.

Example 5-4. app/models.py: Dynamic relationships

```
class Role(db.Model):
    # ...
    users = db.relationship('User', backref='role', lazy='dynamic')
    # ...
```

With the relationship configured in this way, `user_role.users` returns a query that hasn't executed yet, so filters can be added to it:

```
>>> user_role.users.order_by(User.username).all()
[<User u'david'>, <User u'susan'>]
>>> user_role.users.count()
2
```

Database Use in View Functions

The database operations described in the previous sections can be used directly inside view functions. Example 5-5 shows a new version of the home page route that records names entered by users in the database.

Example 5-5. hello.py: Database use in view functions

```
@app.route('/', methods=['GET', 'POST'])
def index():
    form = NameForm()
    if form.validate_on_submit():
        user = User.query.filter_by(username=form.name.data).first()
        if user is None:
            user = User(username = form.name.data)
            db.session.add(user)
            session['known'] = False
        else:
            session['known'] = True
        session['name'] = form.name.data
        form.name.data = ''
        return redirect(url_for('index'))
    return render_template('index.html',
        form = form, name = session.get('name'),
        known = session.get('known', False))
```

In this modified version of the application, each time a name is submitted the application checks for it in the database using the `filter_by()` query filter. A known variable is written to the user session so that after the redirect the information can be sent to the template, where it is used to customize the greeting. Note that for the application to work, the database tables must be created in a Python shell as shown earlier.

The new version of the associated template is shown in Example 5-6. This template uses the known argument to add a second line to the greeting that is different for known and new users.

Example 5-6. templates/index.html

```
{% extends "base.html" %}
{% import "bootstrap/wtf.html" as wtf %}

{% block title %}Flasky{% endblock %}

{% block page_content %}
<div class="page-header">
    <h1>Hello, {% if name %}{{ name }}{% else %}Stranger{% endif %}!</h1>
    {% if not known %}
    <p>Pleased to meet you!</p>
    {% else %}
    <p>Happy to see you again!</p>
    {% endif %}
</div>
{{ wtf.quick_form(form) }}
{% endblock %}
```

 If you have cloned the application's Git repository on GitHub, you can run `git checkout 5b` to check out this version of the application.

Integration with the Python Shell

Having to import the database instance and the models each time a shell session is started is tedious work. To avoid having to constantly repeat these imports, the Flask-Script's shell command can be configured to automatically import certain objects.

To add objects to the import list the shell command needs to be registered with a `make_context` callback function. This is shown in Example 5-7.

Example 5-7. hello.py: Adding a shell context

```
from flask.ext.script import Shell

def make_shell_context():
```

```
    return dict(app=app, db=db, User=User, Role=Role)
manager.add_command("shell", Shell(make_context=make_shell_context))
```

The `make_shell_context()` function registers the application and database instances and the models so that they are automatically imported into the shell:

```
$ python hello.py shell
>>> app
<Flask 'app'>
>>> db
<SQLAlchemy engine='sqlite:////home/flask/flasky/data.sqlite'>
>>> User
<class 'app.User'>
```

 If you have cloned the application's Git repository on GitHub, you can run `git checkout 5c` to check out this version of the application.

Database Migrations with Flask-Migrate

As you make progress developing an application, you will find that your database models need to change, and when that happens the database needs to be updated as well.

Flask-SQLAlchemy creates database tables from models only when they do not exist already, so the only way to make it update tables is by destroying the old tables first, but of course this causes all the data in the database to be lost.

A better solution is to use a *database migration* framework. In the same way source code version control tools keep track of changes to source code files, a database migration framework keeps track of changes to a database *schema*, and then incremental changes can be applied to the database.

The lead developer of SQLAlchemy has written a migration framework called Alembic (*http://bit.ly/alembic-doc*), but instead of using Alembic directly, Flask applications can use the Flask-Migrate (*http://bit.ly/fl-migrate*) extension, a lightweight Alembic wrapper that integrates with Flask-Script to provide all operations through Flask-Script commands.

Creating a Migration Repository

To begin, Flask-Migrate must be installed in the virtual environment:

```
(venv) $ pip install flask-migrate
```

Example 5-8 shows how the extension is initialized.

Example 5-8. hello.py: Flask-Migrate configuration

```
from flask.ext.migrate import Migrate, MigrateCommand

# ...

migrate = Migrate(app, db)
manager.add_command('db', MigrateCommand)
```

To expose the database migration commands, Flask-Migrate exposes a MigrateCommand class that is attached to Flask-Script's manager object. In this example the command is attached using db.

Before database migrations can be maintained, it is necessary to create a migration repository with the init subcommand:

```
(venv) $ python hello.py db init
    Creating directory /home/flask/flasky/migrations...done
    Creating directory /home/flask/flasky/migrations/versions...done
    Generating /home/flask/flasky/migrations/alembic.ini...done
    Generating /home/flask/flasky/migrations/env.py...done
    Generating /home/flask/flasky/migrations/env.pyc...done
    Generating /home/flask/flasky/migrations/README...done
    Generating /home/flask/flasky/migrations/script.py.mako...done
    Please edit configuration/connection/logging settings in
    '/home/flask/flasky/migrations/alembic.ini' before proceeding.
```

This command creates a *migrations* folder, where all the migration scripts will be stored.

The files in a database migration repository must always be added to version control along with the rest of the application.

Creating a Migration Script

In Alembic, a database migration is represented by a *migration script*. This script has two functions called upgrade() and downgrade(). The upgrade() function applies the database changes that are part of the migration, and the downgrade() function removes them. By having the ability to add and remove the changes, Alembic can reconfigure a database to any point in the change history.

Alembic migrations can be created manually or automatically using the revision and migrate commands, respectively. A manual migration creates a migration skeleton script with empty upgrade() and downgrade() functions that need to be implemented by the developer using directives exposed by Alembic's Operations object. An automatic migration, on the other hand, generates the code for the upgrade() and downgrade() functions by looking for differences between the model definitions and the current state of the database.

> Automatic migrations are not always accurate and can miss some details. Migration scripts generated automatically should always be reviewed.

The migrate subcommand creates an automatic migration script:

```
(venv) $ python hello.py db migrate -m "initial migration"
INFO  [alembic.migration] Context impl SQLiteImpl.
INFO  [alembic.migration] Will assume non-transactional DDL.
INFO  [alembic.autogenerate] Detected added table 'roles'
INFO  [alembic.autogenerate] Detected added table 'users'
INFO  [alembic.autogenerate.compare] Detected added index
'ix_users_username' on '['username']'
  Generating /home/flask/flasky/migrations/versions/1bc
  594146bb5_initial_migration.py...done
```

> If you have cloned the application's Git repository on GitHub, you can run git checkout 5d to check out this version of the application. Note that you do not need to generate the migrations for this application as all the migration scripts are included in the repository.

Upgrading the Database

Once a migration script has been reviewed and accepted, it can be applied to the database using the db upgrade command:

```
(venv) $ python hello.py db upgrade
INFO  [alembic.migration] Context impl SQLiteImpl.
INFO  [alembic.migration] Will assume non-transactional DDL.
INFO  [alembic.migration] Running upgrade None -> 1bc594146bb5, initial migration
```

For a first migration, this is effectively equivalent to calling db.create_all(), but in successive migrations the upgrade command applies updates to the tables without affecting their contents.

> If you have cloned the application's Git repository on GitHub, delete your *data.sqlite* database file and then run Flask-Migrate's upgrade command to regenerate the database through the migration framework.

The topic of database design and usage is very important; entire books have been written on the subject. You should consider this chapter as an overview; more advanced topics will be discussed in later chapters. The next chapter is dedicated to sending email.

CHAPTER 6

Email

Many types of applications need to notify users when certain events occur, and the usual method of communication is email. Although the *smtplib* package from the Python standard library can be used to send email inside a Flask application, the Flask-Mail extension wraps smtplib and integrates it nicely with Flask.

Email Support with Flask-Mail

Flask-Mail is installed with pip:

```
(venv) $ pip install flask-mail
```

The extension connects to a Simple Mail Transfer Protocol (SMTP) server and passes emails to it for delivery. If no configuration is given, Flask-Mail connects to *localhost* at port 25 and sends email without authentication. Table 6-1 shows the list of configuration keys that can be used to configure the SMTP server.

Table 6-1. Flask-Mail SMTP server configuration keys

Key	Default	Description
MAIL_HOSTNAME	*localhost*	Hostname or IP address of the email server
MAIL_PORT	25	Port of the email server
MAIL_USE_TLS	False	Enable Transport Layer Security (TLS) security
MAIL_USE_SSL	False	Enable Secure Sockets Layer (SSL) security
MAIL_USERNAME	None	Mail account username
MAIL_PASSWORD	None	Mail account password

During development it may be more convenient to connect to an external SMTP server. As an example, Example 6-1 shows how to configure the application to send email through a Google Gmail account.

Example 6-1. hello.py: Flask-Mail configuration for Gmail

```
import os
# ...
app.config['MAIL_SERVER'] = 'smtp.googlemail.com'
app.config['MAIL_PORT'] = 587
app.config['MAIL_USE_TLS'] = True
app.config['MAIL_USERNAME'] = os.environ.get('MAIL_USERNAME')
app.config['MAIL_PASSWORD'] = os.environ.get('MAIL_PASSWORD')
```

Never write account credentials directly in your scripts, particularly if you plan to release your work as open source. To protect your account information, have your script import sensitive information from the environment.

Flask-Mail is initialized as shown in Example 6-2.

Example 6-2. hello.py: Flask-Mail initialization

```
from flask.ext.mail import Mail
mail = Mail(app)
```

The two environment variables that hold the email server username and password need to be defined in the environment. If you are on Linux or Mac OS X using bash, you can set these variables as follows:

```
(venv) $ export MAIL_USERNAME=<Gmail username>
(venv) $ export MAIL_PASSWORD=<Gmail password>
```

For Microsoft Windows users, the environment variables are set as follows:

```
(venv) $ set MAIL_USERNAME=<Gmail username>
(venv) $ set MAIL_PASSWORD=<Gmail password>
```

Sending Email from the Python Shell

To test the configuration, you can start a shell session and send a test email:

```
(venv) $ python hello.py shell
>>> from flask.ext.mail import Message
>>> from hello import mail
>>> msg = Message('test subject', sender='you@example.com',
...     recipients=['you@example.com'])
>>> msg.body = 'text body'
>>> msg.html = '<b>HTML</b> body'
>>> with app.app_context():
...     mail.send(msg)
...
```

Note that Flask-Mail's `send()` function uses `current_app`, so it needs to be executed with an activated application context.

Integrating Emails with the Application

To avoid having to create email messages manually every time, it is a good idea to abstract the common parts of the application's email sending functionality into a function. As an added benefit, this function can render email bodies from Jinja2 templates to have the most flexibility. The implementation is shown in Example 6-3.

Example 6-3. hello.py: Email support

```
from flask.ext.mail import Message

app.config['FLASKY_MAIL_SUBJECT_PREFIX'] = '[Flasky]'
app.config['FLASKY_MAIL_SENDER'] = 'Flasky Admin <flasky@example.com>'

def send_email(to, subject, template, **kwargs):
    msg = Message(app.config['FLASKY_MAIL_SUBJECT_PREFIX'] + subject,
                  sender=app.config['FLASKY_MAIL_SENDER'], recipients=[to])
    msg.body = render_template(template + '.txt', **kwargs)
    msg.html = render_template(template + '.html', **kwargs)
    mail.send(msg)
```

The function relies on two application-specific configuration keys that define a prefix string for the subject and the address that will be used as sender. The `send_email` function takes the destination address, a subject line, a template for the email body, and a list of keyword arguments. The template name must be given without the extension, so that two versions of the template can be used for the plain- and rich-text bodies. The keyword arguments passed by the caller are given to the `render_template()` calls so that they can be used by the templates that generate the email body.

The `index()` view function can be easily expanded to send an email to the administrator whenever a new name is received with the form. Example 6-4 shows this change.

Example 6-4. hello.py: Email example

```
# ...
app.config['FLASKY_ADMIN'] = os.environ.get('FLASKY_ADMIN')
# ...
@app.route('/', methods=['GET', 'POST'])
def index():
    form = NameForm()
    if form.validate_on_submit():
        user = User.query.filter_by(username=form.name.data).first()
        if user is None:
            user = User(username=form.name.data)
            db.session.add(user)
            session['known'] = False
            if app.config['FLASKY_ADMIN']:
```

```
                send_email(app.config['FLASKY_ADMIN'], 'New User',
                           'mail/new_user', user=user)
        else:
            session['known'] = True
        session['name'] = form.name.data
        form.name.data = ''
        return redirect(url_for('index'))
    return render_template('index.html', form=form, name=session.get('name'),
                           known=session.get('known', False))
```

The recipient of the email is given in the FLASKY_ADMIN environment variable loaded into a configuration variable of the same name during startup. Two template files need to be created for the text and HTML versions of the email. These files are stored in a *mail* subfolder inside *templates* to keep them separate from regular templates. The email templates expect the user to be given as a template argument, so the call to send_email() includes it as a keyword argument.

 If you have cloned the application's Git repository on GitHub, you can run git checkout 6a to check out this version of the application.

In addition to the MAIL_USERNAME and MAIL_PASSWORD environment variables described earlier, this version of the application needs the FLASKY_ADMIN environment variable. For Linux and Mac OS X users, the command to start the application is:

```
(venv) $ export FLASKY_ADMIN=<your-email-address>
```

For Microsoft Windows users, this is the equivalent command:

```
(venv) $ set FLASKY_ADMIN=<Gmail username>
```

With these environment variables set, you can test the application and receive an email every time you enter a new name in the form.

Sending Asynchronous Email

If you sent a few test emails, you likely noticed that the mail.send() function blocks for a few seconds while the email is sent, making the browser look unresponsive during that time. To avoid unnecessary delays during request handling, the email send function can be moved to a background thread. Example 6-5 shows this change.

Example 6-5. hello.py: Asynchronous email support

```
from threading import Thread

def send_async_email(app, msg):
    with app.app_context():
```

```
    mail.send(msg)

def send_email(to, subject, template, **kwargs):
    msg = Message(app.config['FLASKY_MAIL_SUBJECT_PREFIX'] + subject,
                  sender=app.config['FLASKY_MAIL_SENDER'], recipients=[to])
    msg.body = render_template(template + '.txt', **kwargs)
    msg.html = render_template(template + '.html', **kwargs)
    thr = Thread(target=send_async_email, args=[app, msg])
    thr.start()
    return thr
```

This implementation highlights an interesting problem. Many Flask extensions operate under the assumption that there are active application and request contexts. Flask-Mail's `send()` function uses `current_app`, so it requires the application context to be active. But when the `mail.send()` function executes in a different thread, the application context needs to be created artificially using `app.app_context()`.

 If you have cloned the application's Git repository on GitHub, you can run `git checkout 6b` to check out this version of the application.

If you run the application now, you will notice that it is much more responsive, but keep in mind that for applications that send a large volume of email, having a job dedicated to sending email is more appropriate than starting a new thread for every email. For example, the execution of the `send_async_email()` function can be sent to a Celery (*http://www.celeryproject.org/*) task queue.

This chapter completes the overview of the features that are a must-have for most web applications. The problem now is that the *hello.py* script is starting to get large and that makes it harder to work with. In the next chapter, you will learn how to structure a larger application.

CHAPTER 7

Large Application Structure

Although having small web applications stored in a single script can be very convenient, this approach does not scale well. As the application grows in complexity, working with a single large source file becomes problematic.

Unlike most other web frameworks, Flask does not impose a specific organization for large projects; the way to structure the application is left entirely to the developer. In this chapter, a possible way to organize a large application in packages and modules is presented. This structure will be used in the remaining examples of the book.

Project Structure

Example 7-1 shows the basic layout for a Flask application.

Example 7-1. Basic multiple-file Flask application structure

```
|-flasky
  |-app/
    |-templates/
    |-static/
    |-main/
      |-__init__.py
      |-errors.py
      |-forms.py
      |-views.py
    |-__init__.py
    |-email.py
    |-models.py
  |-migrations/
  |-tests/
    |-__init__.py
    |-test*.py
  |-venv/
  |-requirements.txt
```

```
|-config.py
|-manage.py
```

This structure has four top-level folders:

- The Flask application lives inside a package generically named *app*.
- The *migrations* folder contains the database migration scripts, as before.
- Unit tests are written in a *tests* package.
- The *venv* folder contains the Python virtual environment, as before.

There are also a few new files:

- *requirements.txt* lists the package dependencies so that it is easy to regenerate an identical virtual environment on a different computer.
- *config.py* stores the configuration settings.
- *manage.py* launches the application and other application tasks.

To help you fully understand this structure, the following sections describe the process to convert the *hello.py* application to it.

Configuration Options

Applications often need several configuration sets. The best example of this is the need to use different databases during development, testing, and production so that they don't interfere with each other.

Instead of the simple dictionary-like structure configuration used by *hello.py*, a hierarchy of configuration classes can be used. Example 7-2 shows the *config.py* file.

Example 7-2. config.py: Application configuration

```
import os
basedir = os.path.abspath(os.path.dirname(__file__))

class Config:
    SECRET_KEY = os.environ.get('SECRET_KEY') or 'hard to guess string'
    SQLALCHEMY_COMMIT_ON_TEARDOWN = True
    FLASKY_MAIL_SUBJECT_PREFIX = '[Flasky]'
    FLASKY_MAIL_SENDER = 'Flasky Admin <flasky@example.com>'
    FLASKY_ADMIN = os.environ.get('FLASKY_ADMIN')

    @staticmethod
    def init_app(app):
        pass

class DevelopmentConfig(Config):
    DEBUG = True
```

```
    MAIL_SERVER = 'smtp.googlemail.com'
    MAIL_PORT = 587
    MAIL_USE_TLS = True
    MAIL_USERNAME = os.environ.get('MAIL_USERNAME')
    MAIL_PASSWORD = os.environ.get('MAIL_PASSWORD')
    SQLALCHEMY_DATABASE_URI = os.environ.get('DEV_DATABASE_URL') or \
        'sqlite:///' + os.path.join(basedir, 'data-dev.sqlite')

class TestingConfig(Config):
    TESTING = True
    SQLALCHEMY_DATABASE_URI = os.environ.get('TEST_DATABASE_URL') or \
        'sqlite:///' + os.path.join(basedir, 'data-test.sqlite')

class ProductionConfig(Config):
    SQLALCHEMY_DATABASE_URI = os.environ.get('DATABASE_URL') or \
        'sqlite:///' + os.path.join(basedir, 'data.sqlite')

config = {
    'development': DevelopmentConfig,
    'testing': TestingConfig,
    'production': ProductionConfig,

    'default': DevelopmentConfig
}
```

The Config base class contains settings that are common to all configurations; the different subclasses define settings that are specific to a configuration. Additional configurations can be added as needed.

To make configuration more flexible and safe, some settings can be optionally imported from environment variables. For example, the value of the SECRET_KEY, due to its sensitive nature, can be set in the environment, but a default value is provided in case the environment does not define it.

The SQLALCHEMY_DATABASE_URI variable is assigned different values under each of the three configurations. This enables the application to run under different configurations, each using a different database.

Configuration classes can define a init_app() class method that takes an application instance as an argument. Here configuration-specific initialization can performed. For now the base Config class implements an empty init_app() method.

At the bottom of the configuration script, the different configurations are registered in a config dictionary. One of the configurations (the one for development in this case) is also registered as the default.

Application Package

The application package is where all the application code, templates, and static files live. It is called simply *app*, though it can be given an application-specific name if desired. The *templates* and *static* folders are part of the application package, so these two folders are moved inside *app*. The database models and the email support functions are also moved inside this package, each in its own module as *app/models.py* and *app/email.py*.

Using an Application Factory

The way the application is created in the single-file version is very convenient, but it has one big drawback. Because the application is created in the global scope, there is no way to apply configuration changes dynamically: by the time the script is running, the application instance has already been created, so it is already too late to make configuration changes. This is particularly important for unit tests because sometimes it is necessary to run the application under different configuration settings for better test coverage.

The solution to this problem is to delay the creation of the application by moving it into a *factory function* that can be explicitly invoked from the script. This not only gives the script time to set the configuration but also the ability to create multiple application instances—something that can also be very useful during testing. The application factory function, shown in Example 7-3, is defined in the *app* package constructor.

This constructor imports most of the Flask extensions currently in use, but because there is no application instance to initialize them with, it creates them uninitialized by passing no arguments into their constructors. The `create_app()` function is the application factory, which takes as an argument the name of a configuration to use for the application. The configuration settings stored in one of the classes defined in *config.py* can be imported directly into the application using the `from_object()` method available in Flask's `app.config` configuration object. The configuration object is selected by name from the `config` dictionary. Once an application is created and configured, the extensions can be initialized. Calling `init_app()` on the extensions that were created earlier completes their initialization.

Example 7-3. app/__init__.py: Application package constructor

```
from flask import Flask, render_template
from flask.ext.bootstrap import Bootstrap
from flask.ext.mail import Mail
from flask.ext.moment import Moment
from flask.ext.sqlalchemy import SQLAlchemy
from config import config

bootstrap = Bootstrap()
mail = Mail()
moment = Moment()
db = SQLAlchemy()
```

```
def create_app(config_name):
    app = Flask(__name__)
    app.config.from_object(config[config_name])
    config[config_name].init_app(app)

    bootstrap.init_app(app)
    mail.init_app(app)
    moment.init_app(app)
    db.init_app(app)

    # attach routes and custom error pages here

    return app
```

The factory function returns the created application instance, but note that applications created with the factory function in its current state are incomplete, as they are missing routes and custom error page handlers. This is the topic of the next section.

Implementing Application Functionality in a Blueprint

The conversion to an application factory introduces a complication for routes. In single-script applications, the application instance exists in the global scope, so routes can be easily defined using the app.route decorator. But now that the application is created at runtime, the app.route decorator begins to exist only after create_app() is invoked, which is too late. Like routes, custom error page handlers present the same problem, as these are defined with the app.errorhandler decorator.

Luckily Flask offers a better solution using *blueprints*. A blueprint is similar to an application in that it can also define routes. The difference is that routes associated with a blueprint are in a dormant state until the blueprint is registered with an application, at which point the routes become part of it. Using a blueprint defined in the global scope, the routes of the application can be defined in almost the same way as in the single-script application.

Like applications, blueprints can be defined all in a single file or can be created in a more structured way with multiple modules inside a package. To allow for the greatest flexibility, a subpackage inside the application package will be created to host the blueprint. Example 7-4 shows the package constructor, which creates the blueprint.

Example 7-4. app/main/__init__.py: Blueprint creation

```
from flask import Blueprint

main = Blueprint('main', __name__)

from . import views, errors
```

Blueprints are created by instantiating an object of class `Blueprint`. The constructor for this class takes two required arguments: the blueprint name and the module or package where the blueprint is located. As with applications, Python's __name__ variable is in most cases the correct value for the second argument.

The routes of the application are stored in an *app/main/views.py* module inside the package, and the error handlers are in *app/main/errors.py*. Importing these modules causes the routes and error handlers to be associated with the blueprint. It is important to note that the modules are imported at the bottom of the *app/__init__.py* script to avoid circular dependencies, because *views.py* and *errors.py* need to import the `main` blueprint.

The blueprint is registered with the application inside the `create_app()` factory function, as shown in Example 7-5.

Example 7-5. app/_init_.py: Blueprint registration

```
def create_app(config_name):
    # ...

    from main import main as main_blueprint
    app.register_blueprint(main_blueprint)

    return app
```

Example 7-6 shows the error handlers.

Example 7-6. app/main/errors.py: Blueprint with error handlers

```
from flask import render_template
from . import main

@main.app_errorhandler(404)
def page_not_found(e):
    return render_template('404.html'), 404

@main.app_errorhandler(500)
def internal_server_error(e):
    return render_template('500.html'), 500
```

A difference when writing error handlers inside a blueprint is that if the `errorhandler` decorator is used, the handler will only be invoked for errors that originate in the blueprint. To install application-wide error handlers, the `app_errorhandler` must be used instead.

Example 7-7 shows the routes of the application updated to be in the blueprint.

Example 7-7. app/main/views.py: Blueprint with application routes

```
from datetime import datetime
from flask import render_template, session, redirect, url_for
```

```
from . import main
from .forms import NameForm
from .. import db
from ..models import User

@main.route('/', methods=['GET', 'POST'])
def index():
    form = NameForm()
    if form.validate_on_submit():
        # ...
        return redirect(url_for('.index'))
    return render_template('index.html',
                           form=form, name=session.get('name'),
                           known=session.get('known', False),
                           current_time=datetime.utcnow())
```

There are two main differences when writing a view function inside a blueprint. First, as was done for error handlers earlier, the route decorator comes from the blueprint. The second difference is in the usage of the url_for() function. As you may recall, the first argument to this function is the endpoint name of the route, which for application-based routes defaults to the name of the view function. For example, in a single-script application the URL for an index() view function can be obtained with url_for('index').

The difference with blueprints is that Flask applies a namespace to all the endpoints coming from a blueprint so that multiple blueprints can define view functions with the same endpoint names without collisions. The namespace is the name of the blueprint (the first argument to the Blueprint constructor), so the index() view function is registered with endpoint name main.index and its URL can be obtained with url_for('main.index').

The url_for() function also supports a shorter format for endpoints in blueprints in which the blueprint name is omitted, such as url_for('.index'). With this notation, the blueprint for the current request is used. This effectively means that redirects within the same blueprint can use the shorter form, while redirects across blueprints must use the namespaced endpoint name.

To complete the changes to the application page, the form objects are also stored inside the blueprint in an *app/main/forms.py* module.

Launch Script

The *manage.py* file in the top-level folder is used to start the application. This script is shown in Example 7-8.

Example 7-8. manage.py: Launch script

```python
#!/usr/bin/env python
import os
from app import create_app, db
from app.models import User, Role
from flask.ext.script import Manager, Shell
from flask.ext.migrate import Migrate, MigrateCommand

app = create_app(os.getenv('FLASK_CONFIG') or 'default')
manager = Manager(app)
migrate = Migrate(app, db)

def make_shell_context():
    return dict(app=app, db=db, User=User, Role=Role)
manager.add_command("shell", Shell(make_context=make_shell_context))
manager.add_command('db', MigrateCommand)

if __name__ == '__main__':
    manager.run()
```

The script begins by creating an application. The configuration used is taken from the environment variable FLASK_CONFIG if it's defined; if not, the default configuration is used. Flask-Script, Flask-Migrate, and the custom context for the Python shell are then initialized.

As a convenience, a shebang line is added, so that on Unix-based operating systems the script can be executed as ./manage.py instead of the more verbose python manage.py.

Requirements File

Applications must include a *requirements.txt* file that records all the package dependencies, with the exact version numbers. This is important in case the virtual environment needs to be regenerated in a different machine, such as the machine on which the application will be deployed for production use. This file can be generated automatically by pip with the following command:

```
(venv) $ pip freeze >requirements.txt
```

It is a good idea to refresh this file whenever a package is installed or upgraded. An example requirements file is shown here:

```
Flask==0.10.1
Flask-Bootstrap==3.0.3.1
Flask-Mail==0.9.0
Flask-Migrate==1.1.0
Flask-Moment==0.2.0
Flask-SQLAlchemy==1.0
Flask-Script==0.6.6
Flask-WTF==0.9.4
```

```
Jinja2==2.7.1
Mako==0.9.1
MarkupSafe==0.18
SQLAlchemy==0.8.4
WTForms==1.0.5
Werkzeug==0.9.4
alembic==0.6.2
blinker==1.3
itsdangerous==0.23
```

When you need to build a perfect replica of the virtual environment, you can create a new virtual environment and run the following command on it:

```
(venv) $ pip install -r requirements.txt
```

The version numbers in the example *requirements.txt* file are likely going to be outdated by the time you read this. You can try using more recent releases of the packages, if you like. If you experience any problems, you can always go back to the versions specified in the requirements file, as those are known to be compatible with the application.

Unit Tests

This application is very small so there isn't a lot to test yet, but as an example two simple tests can be defined as shown in Example 7-9.

Example 7-9. tests/test_basics.py: Unit tests

```
import unittest
from flask import current_app
from app import create_app, db

class BasicsTestCase(unittest.TestCase):
    def setUp(self):
        self.app = create_app('testing')
        self.app_context = self.app.app_context()
        self.app_context.push()
        db.create_all()

    def tearDown(self):
        db.session.remove()
        db.drop_all()
        self.app_context.pop()

    def test_app_exists(self):
        self.assertFalse(current_app is None)

    def test_app_is_testing(self):
        self.assertTrue(current_app.config['TESTING'])
```

The tests are written using the standard `unittest` package from the Python standard library. The `setUp()` and `tearDown()` methods run before and after each test, and any methods that have a name that begins with `test_` are executed as tests.

 If you want to learn more about writing unit tests with Python's *unittest* package, read the official documentation (*http://bit.ly/py-unittest*).

The `setUp()` method tries to create an environment for the test that is close to that of a running application. It first creates an application configured for testing and activates its context. This step ensures that tests have access to `current_app`, like regular requests. Then it creates a brand-new database that the test can use when necessary. The database and the application context are removed in the `tearDown()` method.

The first test ensures that the application instance exists. The second test ensures that the application is running under the testing configuration. To make the *tests* folder a proper package, a *tests/__init__.py* file needs to be added, but this can be an empty file, as the `unittest` package can scan all the modules and locate the tests.

 If you have cloned the application's Git repository on GitHub, you can run `git checkout 7a` to check out the converted version of the application. To ensure that you have all the dependencies installed, also run `pip install -r requirements.txt`.

To run the unit tests, a custom command can be added to the *manage.py* script. Example 7-10 shows how to add a `test` command.

Example 7-10. manage.py: Unit test launcher command

```
@manager.command
def test():
    """Run the unit tests."""
    import unittest
    tests = unittest.TestLoader().discover('tests')
    unittest.TextTestRunner(verbosity=2).run(tests)
```

The `manager.command` decorator makes it simple to implement custom commands. The name of the decorated function is used as the command name, and the function's docstring is displayed in the help messages. The implementation of `test()` function invokes the test runner from the `unittest` package.

The unit tests can be executed as follows:

```
(venv) $ python manage.py test
test_app_exists (test_basics.BasicsTestCase) ... ok
test_app_is_testing (test_basics.BasicsTestCase) ... ok

.-----------------------------------------------------------------
Ran 2 tests in 0.001s

OK
```

Database Setup

The restructured application uses a different database than the single-script version.

The database URL is taken from an environment variable as a first choice, with a default SQLite database as an alternative. The environment variables and SQLite database filenames are different for each of the three configurations. For example, in the development configuration the URL is obtained from environment variable DEV_DATABASE_URL, and if that is not defined then a SQLite database with the name *data-dev.sqlite* is used.

Regardless of the source of the database URL, the database tables must be created for the new database. When working with Flask-Migrate to keep track of migrations, database tables can be created or upgraded to the latest revision with a single command:

```
(venv) $ python manage.py db upgrade
```

Believe it or not, you have reached the end of Part I. You now have learned the basic elements necessary to build a web application with Flask, but you probably feel unsure about how all these pieces fit together to form a real application. The goal of Part II is to help with that by walking you through the development of a complete application.

## PART II

Example: A Social Blogging Application

CHAPTER 8

User Authentication

Most applications need to keep track of who its users are. When users connect with the application, they *authenticate* with it, a process by which they make their identity known. Once the application knows who the user is, it can offer a customized experience.

The most commonly used method of authentication requires users to provide a piece of identification (either their email or username) and a secret password. In this chapter, the complete authentication system for Flasky is created.

Authentication Extensions for Flask

There are many excellent Python authentication packages, but none of them do everything. The user authentication solution presented in this chapter uses several packages and provides the glue that makes them work well together. This is the list of packages that will be used:

- Flask-Login: Management of user sessions for logged-in users
- Werkzeug: Password hashing and verification
- itsdangerous: Cryptographically secure token generation and verification

In addition to authentication-specific packages, the following general-purpose extensions will be used:

- Flask-Mail: Sending of authentication-related emails
- Flask-Bootstrap: HTML templates
- Flask-WTF: Web forms

Password Security

The safety of user information stored in databases is often overlooked during the design of web applications. If an attacker is able to break into your server and access your user database, then you risk the security of your users, and the risk is bigger than you think. It is a known fact that most users use the same password on multiple sites, so even if you don't store any sensitive information, access to the passwords stored in your database can give the attacker access to accounts your users have on other sites.

The key to storing user passwords securely in a database relies not on storing the password itself but a *hash* of it. A password hashing function takes a password as input and applies one or more cryptographic transformations to it. The result is a new sequence of characters that has no resemblance to the original password. Password hashes can be verified in place of the real passwords because hashing functions are repeatable: given the same inputs, the result is always the same.

 Password hashing is a complex task that is hard to get right. It is recommended that you don't implement your own solution but instead rely on reputable libraries that have been reviewed by the community. If you are interested in learning what's involved in generating secure password hashes, the article Salted Password Hashing - Doing it Right (*http://bit.ly/saltedpass*) is a worthwhile read.

Hashing Passwords with Werkzeug

Werkzeug's *security* module conveniently implements secure password hashing. This functionality is exposed with just two functions, used in the registration and verification phases, respectively:

- `generate_password_hash(password, method=pbkdf2:sha1, salt_length=8)`: This function takes a plain-text password and returns the password hash as a string that can be stored in the user database. The default values for `method` and `salt_length` are sufficient for most use cases.

- `check_password_hash(hash, password)`: This function takes a password hash retrieved from the database and the password entered by the user. A return value of `True` indicates that the password is correct.

Example 8-1 shows the changes to the `User` model created in Chapter 5 to accommodate password hashing.

Example 8-1. app/models.py: Password hashing in User model

```
from werkzeug.security import generate_password_hash, check_password_hash
```

```
class User(db.Model):
    # ...
    password_hash = db.Column(db.String(128))

    @property
    def password(self):
        raise AttributeError('password is not a readable attribute')

    @password.setter
    def password(self, password):
        self.password_hash = generate_password_hash(password)

    def verify_password(self, password):
        return check_password_hash(self.password_hash, password)
```

The password hashing function is implemented through a write-only property called password. When this property is set, the setter method will call Werkzeug's generate_password_hash() function and write the result to the password_hash field. Attempting to read the password property will return an error, as clearly the original password cannot be recovered once hashed.

The verify_password method takes a password and passes it to Werkzeug's check_password_hash() function for verification against the hashed version stored in the User model. If this method returns True, then the password is correct.

 If you have cloned the application's Git repository on GitHub, you can run git checkout 8a to check out this version of the application.

The password hashing functionality is now complete and can be tested in the shell:

```
(venv) $ python manage.py shell
>>> u = User()
>>> u.password = 'cat'
>>> u.password_hash
'pbkdf2:sha1:1000$duxMk0OF$4735b293e397d6eeaf650aaf490fd9091f928bed'
>>> u.verify_password('cat')
True
>>> u.verify_password('dog')
False
>>> u2 = User()
>>> u2.password = 'cat'
>>> u2.password_hash
'pbkdf2:sha1:1000$UjvnGeTP$875e28eb0874f44101d6b332442218f66975ee89'
```

Note how users u and u2 have completely different password hashes, even though they both use the same password. To ensure that this functionality continues to work in the future, the above tests can be written as unit tests that can be repeated easily. In Example 8-2 a new module inside the *tests* package is shown with three new tests that exercise the recent changes to the User model.

Example 8-2. tests/test_user_model.py: Password hashing tests

```python
import unittest
from app.models import User

class UserModelTestCase(unittest.TestCase):
    def test_password_setter(self):
        u = User(password = 'cat')
        self.assertTrue(u.password_hash is not None)

    def test_no_password_getter(self):
        u = User(password = 'cat')
        with self.assertRaises(AttributeError):
            u.password

    def test_password_verification(self):
        u = User(password = 'cat')
        self.assertTrue(u.verify_password('cat'))
        self.assertFalse(u.verify_password('dog'))

    def test_password_salts_are_random(self):
        u = User(password='cat')
        u2 = User(password='cat')
        self.assertTrue(u.password_hash != u2.password_hash)
```

Creating an Authentication Blueprint

Blueprints were introduced in Chapter 7 as a way to define routes in the global scope after the creation of the application was moved into a factory function. The routes related to the user authentication system can be added to a auth blueprint. Using different blueprints for different sets of application functionality is a great way to keep the code neatly organized.

The auth blueprint will be hosted in a Python package with the same name. The blueprint's package constructor creates the blueprint object and imports routes from a *views.py* module. This is shown in Example 8-3.

Example 8-3. app/auth/__init__.py: Blueprint creation

```python
from flask import Blueprint

auth = Blueprint('auth', __name__)

from . import views
```

The *app/auth/views.py* module, shown in Example 8-4, imports the blueprint and defines the routes associated with authentication using its `route` decorator. For now a */login* route is added, which renders a placeholder template of the same name.

Example 8-4. app/auth/views.py: Blueprint routes and view functions

```
from flask import render_template
from . import auth

@auth.route('/login')
def login():
    return render_template('auth/login.html')
```

Note that the template file given to `render_template()` is stored inside the *auth* folder. This folder must be created inside *app/templates*, as Flask expects the templates to be relative to the application's template folder. By storing the blueprint templates in their own folder, there is no risk of naming collisions with the `main` blueprint or any other blueprints that will be added in the future.

 Blueprints can also be configured to have their own independent folder for templates. When multiple template folders have been configured, the `render_template()` function searches the templates folder configured for the application first and then searches the template folders defined by blueprints.

The `auth` blueprint needs to be attached to the application in the `create_app()` factory function as shown in Example 8-5.

Example 8-5. app/__init__.py: Blueprint attachment

```
def create_app(config_name):
    # ...
    from .auth import auth as auth_blueprint
    app.register_blueprint(auth_blueprint, url_prefix='/auth')

    return app
```

The `url_prefix` argument in the blueprint registration is optional. When used, all the routes defined in the blueprint will be registered with the given prefix, in this case */auth*. For example, the */login* route will be registered as */auth/login*, and the fully qualified URL under the development web server then becomes *http://localhost:5000/auth/login*.

If you have cloned the application's Git repository on GitHub, you can run `git checkout 8b` to check out this version of the application.

User Authentication with Flask-Login

When users log in to the application, their authenticated state has to be recorded so that it is remembered as they navigate through different pages. Flask-Login is a small but extremely useful extension that specializes in managing this particular aspect of a user authentication system, without being tied to a specific authentication mechanism.

To begin, the extension needs to be installed in the virtual environment:

```
(venv) $ pip install flask-login
```

Preparing the User Model for Logins

To be able to work with the application's User model, the Flask-Login extension requires a few methods to be implemented by it. The required methods are shown in Table 8-1.

Table 8-1. Flask-Login user methods

Method	Description
is_authenticated()	Must return True if the user has login credentials or False otherwise.
is_active()	Must return True if the user is allowed to log in or False otherwise. A False return value can be used for disabled accounts.
is_anonymous()	Must always return False for regular users.
get_id()	Must return a unique identifier for the user, encoded as a Unicode string.

These four methods can be implemented directly as methods in the model class, but as an easier alternative Flask-Login provides a UserMixin class that has default implementations that are appropriate for most cases. The updated User model is shown in Example 8-6.

Example 8-6. app/models.py: Updates to the User model to support user logins

```
from flask.ext.login import UserMixin

class User(UserMixin, db.Model):
    __tablename__ = 'users'
    id = db.Column(db.Integer, primary_key = True)
    email = db.Column(db.String(64), unique=True, index=True)
    username = db.Column(db.String(64), unique=True, index=True)
    password_hash = db.Column(db.String(128))
    role_id = db.Column(db.Integer, db.ForeignKey('roles.id'))
```

Note that an `email` field was also added. In this application, users will log in with their email, as they are less likely to forget their email addresses than their usernames.

Flask-Login is initialized in the application factory function, as shown in Example 8-7.

Example 8-7. app/__init__.py: Flask-Login initialization

```
from flask.ext.login import LoginManager

login_manager = LoginManager()
login_manager.session_protection = 'strong'
login_manager.login_view = 'auth.login'

def create_app(config_name):
    # ...
    login_manager.init_app(app)
    # ...
```

The `session_protection` attribute of the `LoginManager` object can be set to `None`, `'basic'`, or `'strong'` to provide different levels of security against user session tampering. With the `'strong'` setting, Flask-Login will keep track of the client's IP address and browser agent and will log the user out if it detects a change. The `login_view` attribute sets the endpoint for the login page. Recall that because the login route is inside a blueprint, it needs to be prefixed with the blueprint name.

Finally, Flask-Login requires the application to set up a callback function that loads a user, given the identifier. This function is shown in Example 8-8.

Example 8-8. app/models.py: User loader callback function

```
from . import login_manager

@login_manager.user_loader
def load_user(user_id):
    return User.query.get(int(user_id))
```

The user loader callback function receives a user identifier as a Unicode string. The return value of the function must be the user object if available or `None` otherwise.

Protecting Routes

To protect a route so that it can only be accessed by authenticated users, Flask-Login provides a `login_required` decorator. An example of its usage follows:

```
from flask.ext.login import login_required

@app.route('/secret')
@login_required
def secret():
    return 'Only authenticated users are allowed!'
```

If this route is accessed by a user who is not authenticated, Flask-Login will intercept the request and send the user to the login page instead.

Adding a Login Form

The login form that will be presented to users has a text field for the email address, a password field, a "remember me" checkbox, and a submit button. The Flask-WTF form class is shown in Example 8-9.

Example 8-9. app/auth/forms.py: Login form

```
from flask.ext.wtf import Form
from wtforms import StringField, PasswordField, BooleanField, SubmitField
from wtforms.validators import Required, Email

class LoginForm(Form):
    email = StringField('Email', validators=[Required(), Length(1, 64),
                                             Email()])
    password = PasswordField('Password', validators=[Required()])
    remember_me = BooleanField('Keep me logged in')
    submit = SubmitField('Log In')
```

The email field takes advantage of the `Length()` and `Email()` validators provided by WTForms. The `PasswordField` class represents an `<input>` element with `type="password"`. The `BooleanField` class represents a checkbox.

The template associated with the login page is stored in *auth/login.html*. This template just needs to render the form using Flask-Bootstrap's `wtf.quick_form()` macro. Figure 8-1 shows the login form rendered by the web browser.

The navigation bar in the *base.html* template uses a Jinja2 conditional to display "Sign In" or "Sign Out" links depending on the logged in state of the current user. The conditional is shown in Example 8-10.

Example 8-10. app/templates/base.html: Sign In and Sign Out navigation bar links

```
<ul class="nav navbar-nav navbar-right">
    {% if current_user.is_authenticated() %}
    <li><a href="{{ url_for('auth.logout') }}">Sign Out</a></li>
    {% else %}
    <li><a href="{{ url_for('auth.login') }}">Sign In</a></li>
    {% endif %}
</ul>
```

The `current_user` variable used in the conditional is defined by Flask-Login and is automatically available to view functions and templates. This variable contains the user currently logged in, or a proxy anonymous user object if the user is not logged in. Anonymous user objects respond to the `is_authenticated()` method with `False`, so this is a convenient way to know whether the current user is logged in.

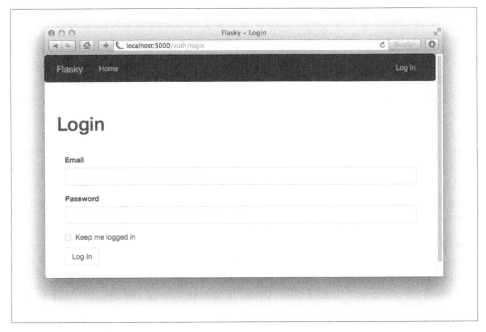

Figure 8-1. Login form

Signing Users In

The implementation of the login() view function is shown in Example 8-11.

Example 8-11. app/auth/views.py: Sign In route

```python
from flask import render_template, redirect, request, url_for, flash
from flask.ext.login import login_user
from . import auth
from ..models import User
from .forms import LoginForm

@auth.route('/login', methods=['GET', 'POST'])
def login():
    form = LoginForm()
    if form.validate_on_submit():
        user = User.query.filter_by(email=form.email.data).first()
        if user is not None and user.verify_password(form.password.data):
            login_user(user, form.remember_me.data)
            return redirect(request.args.get('next') or url_for('main.index'))
        flash('Invalid username or password.')
    return render_template('auth/login.html', form=form)
```

The view function creates a LoginForm object and uses it like the simple form in Chapter 4. When the request is of type GET, the view function just renders the template, which in turn displays the form. When the form is submitted in a POST request Flask-WTF's validate_on_submit() function validates the form variables, and then attempts to log the user in.

To log a user in, the function begins by loading the user from the database using the email provided with the form. If a user with the given email address exists, then its verify_password() method is called with the password that also came with the form. If the password is valid, Flask-Login's login_user() function is invoked to record the user as logged in for the user session. The login_user() function takes the user to log in and an optional "remember me" Boolean, which was also submitted with the form. A value of False for this argument causes the user session to expire when the browser window is closed, so the user will have to log in again next time. A value of True causes a long-term cookie to be set in the user's browser and with that the user session can be restored.

In accordance with the Post/Redirect/Get pattern discussed in Chapter 4, the POST request that submitted the login credentials ends with a redirect, but there are two possible URL destinations. If the login form was presented to the user to prevent un-authorized access to a protected URL, then Flask-Login saved the original URL in the next query string argument, which can be accessed from the request.args dictionary. If the next query string argument is not available, a redirect to the home page is issued instead. If the email or the password provided by the user are invalid, a flash message is set and the form is rendered again for the user to retry.

 On a production server, the login route must be made available over secure HTTP so that the form data transmitted to the server is en-crypted. Without secure HTTP, the login credentials can be intercep-ted during transit, defeating any efforts put into securing passwords in the server.

The login template needs to be updated to render the form. These changes are shown in Example 8-12.

Example 8-12. app/templates/auth/login.html: Render login form

```
{% extends "base.html" %}
{% import "bootstrap/wtf.html" as wtf %}

{% block title %}Flasky - Login{% endblock %}

{% block page_content %}
<div class="page-header">
    <h1>Login</h1>
</div>
<div class="col-md-4">
    {{ wtf.quick_form(form) }}
```

```
</div>
{% endblock %}
```

Signing Users Out

The implementation of the logout route is shown in Example 8-13.

Example 8-13. app/auth/views.py: Sign Out route

```
from flask.ext.login import logout_user, login_required

@auth.route('/logout')
@login_required
def logout():
    logout_user()
    flash('You have been logged out.')
    return redirect(url_for('main.index'))
```

To log a user out, Flask-Login's logout_user() function is called to remove and reset the user session. The logout is completed with a flash message that confirms the action and a redirect to the home page.

 If you have cloned the application's Git repository on GitHub, you can run git checkout 8c to check out this version of the application. This update contains a database migration, so remember to run python manage.py db upgrade after you check out the code. To ensure that you have all the dependencies installed, also run pip install -r requirements.txt.

Testing Logins

To verify that the login functionality is working, the home page can be updated to greet the logged-in user by name. The template section that generates the greeting is shown in Example 8-14.

Example 8-14. app/templates/index.html: Greet the logged-in user

```
Hello,
{% if current_user.is_authenticated() %}
    {{ current_user.username }}
{% else %}
    Stranger
{% endif %}!
```

In this template once again current_user.is_authenticated() is used to determine whether the user is logged in.

Because no user registration functionality has been built, a new user can be registered from the shell:

```
(venv) $ python manage.py shell
>>> u = User(email='john@example.com', username='john', password='cat')
>>> db.session.add(u)
>>> db.session.commit()
```

The user created previously can now log in. Figure 8-2 shows the application home page
with the user logged in.

Figure 8-2. Home page after successful login

New User Registration

When new users want to become members of the application, they must register with
it so that they are known and can log in. A link in the login page will send them to a
registration page, where they can enter their email address, username, and password.

Adding a User Registration Form

The form that will be used in the registration page asks the user to enter an email address,
username, and password. This form is shown in Example 8-15.

Example 8-15. app/auth/forms.py: User registration form

```
from flask.ext.wtf import Form
from wtforms import StringField, PasswordField, BooleanField, SubmitField
from wtforms.validators import Required, Length, Email, Regexp, EqualTo
```

```
from wtforms import ValidationError
from ..models import User

class RegistrationForm(Form):
    email = StringField('Email', validators=[Required(), Length(1, 64),
                                             Email()])
    username = StringField('Username', validators=[
        Required(), Length(1, 64), Regexp('^[A-Za-z][A-Za-z0-9_.]*$', 0,
                                          'Usernames must have only letters, '
                                          'numbers, dots or underscores')])
    password = PasswordField('Password', validators=[
        Required(), EqualTo('password2', message='Passwords must match.')])
    password2 = PasswordField('Confirm password', validators=[Required()])
    submit = SubmitField('Register')

    def validate_email(self, field):
        if User.query.filter_by(email=field.data).first():
            raise ValidationError('Email already registered.')

    def validate_username(self, field):
        if User.query.filter_by(username=field.data).first():
            raise ValidationError('Username already in use.')
```

This form uses the Regexp validator from WTForms to ensure that the username field contains letters, numbers, underscores, and dots only. The two arguments to the validator that follow the regular expression are the regular expression flags and the error message to display on failure.

The password is entered twice as a safety measure, but this step makes it necessary to validate that the two password fields have the same content, which is done with another validator from WTForms called EqualTo. This validator is attached to one of the password fields with the name of the other field given as an argument.

This form also has two custom validators implemented as methods. When a form defines a method with the prefix validate_ followed by the name of a field, the method is invoked in addition to any regularly defined validators. In this case, the custom validators for email and username ensure that the values given are not duplicates. The custom validators indicate a validation error by throwing a ValidationError exception with the text of the error message as argument.

The template that presents this format is called /templates/auth/register.html. Like the login template, this one also renders the form with wtf.quick_form(). The registration page is shown in Figure 8-3.

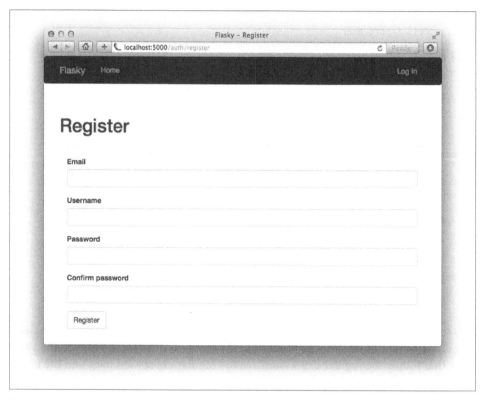

Figure 8-3. New user registration form

The registration page needs to be linked from the login page so that users who don't have an account can easily find it. This change is shown in Example 8-16.

Example 8-16. app/templates/auth/login.html: Link to the registration page

```
<p>
    New user?
    <a href="{{ url_for('auth.register') }}">
        Click here to register
    </a>
</p>
```

Registering New Users

Handling user registrations does not present any big surprises. When the registration form is submitted and validated, a new user is added to the database using the user-provided information. The view function that performs this task is shown in Example 8-17.

Example 8-17. app/auth/views.py: User registration route

```python
@auth.route('/register', methods=['GET', 'POST'])
def register():
    form = RegistrationForm()
    if form.validate_on_submit():
        user = User(email=form.email.data,
                    username=form.username.data,
                    password=form.password.data)
        db.session.add(user)
        flash('You can now login.')
        return redirect(url_for('auth.login'))
    return render_template('auth/register.html', form=form)
```

 If you have cloned the application's Git repository on GitHub, you can run `git checkout 8d` to check out this version of the application.

Account Confirmation

For certain types of applications, it is important to ensure that the user information provided during registration is valid. A common requirement is to ensure that the user can be reached through the provided email address.

To validate the email address, applications send a confirmation email to users immediately after they register. The new account is initially marked as unconfirmed until the instructions in the email are followed, which proves that the user can be reached. The account confirmation procedure usually involves clicking a specially crafted URL link that includes a confirmation token.

Generating Confirmation Tokens with itsdangerous

The simplest account confirmation link would be a URL with the format *http://www.example.com/auth/confirm/<id>* included in the confirmation email, where *id* is the numeric `id` assigned to the user in the database. When the user clicks the link, the view function that handles this route receives the user `id` to confirm as an argument and can easily update the confirmed status of the user.

But this is obviously not a secure implementation, as any user who figures out the format of the confirmation links will be able to confirm arbitrary accounts just by sending random numbers in the URL. The idea is to replace the *id* in the URL with a token that contains the same information securely encrypted.

If you recall the discussion on user sessions in Chapter 4, Flask uses cryptographically signed cookies to protect the content of user sessions against tampering. These secure cookies are signed by a package called *itsdangerous*. The same idea can be applied to confirmation tokens.

The following is a short shell session that shows how itsdangerous can generate a secure token that contains a user id inside:

```
(venv) $ python manage.py shell
>>> from manage import app
>>> from itsdangerous import TimedJSONWebSignatureSerializer as Serializer
>>> s = Serializer(app.config['SECRET_KEY'], expires_in = 3600)
>>> token = s.dumps({ 'confirm': 23 })
>>> token
'eyJhbGciOiJIUzI1NiIsImV4cCI6MTM4MTcxODU1OCwiaWF0IjoxMzgxNzE0OTU4fQ.ey ...'
>>> data = s.loads(token)
>>> data
{u'confirm': 23}
```

Itsdangerous provides several types of token generators. Among them, the class `TimedJSONWebSignatureSerializer` generates JSON Web Signatures (JWS) with a time expiration. The constructor of this class takes an encryption key as argument, which in a Flask application can be the configured SECRET_KEY.

The `dumps()` method generates a cryptographic signature for the data given as an argument and then serializes the data plus the signature as a convenient token string. The `expires_in` argument sets an expiration time for the token expressed in seconds.

To decode the token, the serializer object provides a `loads()` method that takes the token as its only argument. The function verifies the signature and the expiration time and, if found valid, it returns the original data. When the `loads()` method is given an invalid token or a valid token that is expired, an exception is thrown.

Token generation and verification using this functionality can be added to the `User` model. The changes are shown in Example 8-18.

Example 8-18. app/models.py: User account confirmation

```
from itsdangerous import TimedJSONWebSignatureSerializer as Serializer
from flask import current_app
from . import db

class User(UserMixin, db.Model):
    # ...
    confirmed = db.Column(db.Boolean, default=False)

    def generate_confirmation_token(self, expiration=3600):
        s = Serializer(current_app.config['SECRET_KEY'], expiration)
        return s.dumps({'confirm': self.id})

    def confirm(self, token):
        s = Serializer(current_app.config['SECRET_KEY'])
        try:
```

```
        data = s.loads(token)
    except:
        return False
    if data.get('confirm') != self.id:
        return False
    self.confirmed = True
    db.session.add(self)
    return True
```

The generate_confirmation_token() method generates a token with a default validity time of one hour. The confirm() method verifies the token and, if valid, sets the new confirmed attribute to True.

In addition to verifying the token, the confirm() function checks that the id from the token matches the logged-in user, which is stored in current_user. This ensures that even if a malicious user figures out how to generate signed tokens, he or she cannot confirm somebody else's account.

 Because a new column was added to the model to track the confirmed state of each account, a new database migration needs to be generated and applied.

The two new methods added to the User model are easily tested in unit tests. You can find the unit tests in the GitHub repository for the application.

Sending Confirmation Emails

The current */register* route redirects to */index* after adding the new user to the database. Before redirecting, this route now needs to send the confirmation email. This change is shown in Example 8-19.

Example 8-19. app/auth/views.py: Registration route with confirmation email

```
from ..email import send_email

@auth.route('/register', methods = ['GET', 'POST'])
def register():
    form = RegistrationForm()
    if form.validate_on_submit():
        # ...
        db.session.add(user)
        db.session.commit()
        token = user.generate_confirmation_token()
        send_email(user.email, 'Confirm Your Account',
                   'auth/email/confirm', user=user, token=token)
        flash('A confirmation email has been sent to you by email.')
```

```
        return redirect(url_for('main.index'))
    return render_template('auth/register.html', form=form)
```

Note that a `db.session.commit()` call had to be added, even though the application configured automatic database commits at the end of the request. The problem is that new users get assigned an `id` when they are committed to the database. Because the `id` is needed for the confirmation token, the commit cannot be delayed.

The email templates used by the authentication blueprint will be added in the folder *templates/auth/email* to keep them separate from the HTML templates. As discussed in Chapter 6, for each email two templates are needed for the plain- and rich-text versions of the body. As an example, Example 8-20 shows the plain-text version of the confirmation email template, and you can find the equivalent HTML version in the GitHub repository.

Example 8-20. app/auth/templates/auth/email/confirm.txt: Text body of confirmation email

```
Dear {{ user.username }},

Welcome to Flasky!

To confirm your account please click on the following link:

{{ url_for('auth.confirm', token=token, _external=True) }}

Sincerely,

The Flasky Team

Note: replies to this email address are not monitored.
```

By default, `url_for()` generates relative URLs, so, for example, `url_for('auth.confirm', token='abc')` returns the string `'/auth/confirm/abc'`. This, of course, is not a valid URL that can be sent in an email. Relative URLs work fine when they are used within the context of a web page because the browser converts them to absolute by adding the hostname and port number from the current page, but when sending a URL over email there is no such context. The `_external=True` argument is added to the `url_for()` call to request a fully qualified URL that includes the scheme (*http://* or *https://*), hostname, and port.

The view function that confirms accounts is shown in Example 8-21.

Example 8-21. app/auth/views.py: Confirm a user account

```
from flask.ext.login import current_user

@auth.route('/confirm/<token>')
@login_required
```

```
def confirm(token):
    if current_user.confirmed:
        return redirect(url_for('main.index'))
    if current_user.confirm(token):
        flash('You have confirmed your account. Thanks!')
    else:
        flash('The confirmation link is invalid or has expired.')
    return redirect(url_for('main.index'))
```

This route is protected with the login_required decorator from Flask-Login, so that when the users click on the link from the confirmation email they are asked to log in before they reach this view function.

The function first checks if the logged-in user is already confirmed, and in that case it redirects to the home page, as obviously there is nothing to do. This can prevent unnecessary work if a user clicks the confirmation token multiple times by mistake.

Because the actual token confirmation is done entirely in the User model, all the view function needs to do is call the confirm() method and then flash a message according to the result. When the confirmation succeeds, the User model's confirmed attribute is changed and added to the session, which will be committed when the request ends.

Each application can decide what unconfirmed users are allowed to do before they confirm their account. One possibility is to allow unconfirmed users to log in, but only show them a page that asks them to confirm their accounts before they can gain access.

This step can be done using Flask's before_request hook, which was briefly described in Chapter 2. From a blueprint, the before_request hook applies only to requests that belong to the blueprint. To install a hook for all application requests from a blueprint, the before_app_request decorator must be used instead. Example 8-22 shows how this handler is implemented.

Example 8-22. app/auth/views.py: Filter unconfirmed accounts in before_app_request handler

```
@auth.before_app_request
def before_request():
    if current_user.is_authenticated() \
            and not current_user.confirmed \
            and request.endpoint[:5] != 'auth.':
        return redirect(url_for('auth.unconfirmed'))


@auth.route('/unconfirmed')
def unconfirmed():
    if current_user.is_anonymous() or current_user.confirmed:
        return redirect('main.index')
    return render_template('auth/unconfirmed.html')
```

The `before_app_request` handler will intercept a request when three conditions are true:

1. A user is logged in (`current_user.is_authenticated()` must return `True`).
2. The account for the user is not confirmed.
3. The requested endpoint (accessible as `request.endpoint`) is outside of the authentication blueprint. Access to the authentication routes needs to be granted, as those are the routes that will enable the user to confirm the account or perform other account management functions.

If the three conditions are met, then a redirect is issued to a new */auth/unconfirmed* route that shows a page with information about account confirmation.

When a `before_request` or `before_app_request` callback returns a response or a redirect, Flask sends that to the client without invoking the view function associated with the request. This effectively allows these callbacks to intercept a request when necessary.

The page that is presented to unconfirmed users (shown in Figure 8-4) just renders a template that gives users instructions for how to confirm their account and offers a link to request a new confirmation email, in case the original email was lost. The route that resends the confirmation email is shown in Example 8-23.

Example 8-23. app/auth/views.py: Resend account confirmation email

```
@auth.route('/confirm')
@login_required
def resend_confirmation():
    token = current_user.generate_confirmation_token()
    send_email('auth/email/confirm',
               'Confirm Your Account', user, token=token)
    flash('A new confirmation email has been sent to you by email.')
    return redirect(url_for('main.index'))
```

This route repeats what was done in the registration route using `current_user`, the user who is logged in, as the target user. This route is also protected with `login_required` to ensure that when it is accessed, the user that is making the request is known.

If you have cloned the application's Git repository on GitHub, you can run `git checkout 8e` to check out this version of the application. This update contains a database migration, so remember to run `python manage.py db upgrade` after you check out the code.

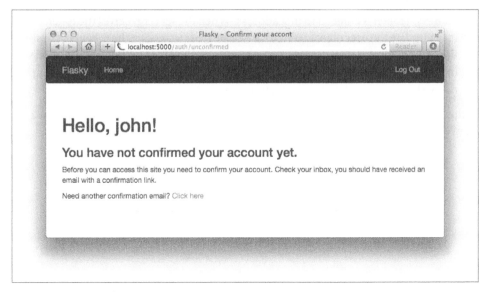

Figure 8-4. Unconfirmed account page

Account Management

Users who have accounts with the application may need to make changes to their accounts from time to time. The following tasks can be added to the authentication blueprint using the techniques presented in this chapter:

Password updates

Security conscious users may want to change their passwords periodically. This is an easy feature to implement, because as long as the user is logged in, it is safe to present a form that asks for the old password and a new password to replace it. (This feature is implemented as commit 8f in the GitHub repository.)

Password resets

To avoid locking users out of the application when they forget their passwords, a password reset option can be offered. To implement password resets in a secure way, it is necessary to use tokens similar to those used to confirm accounts. When a user requests a password reset, an email with a reset token is sent to the registered email address. The user then clicks the link in the email and, after the token is verified, a form is presented where a new password can be entered. (This feature is implemented as commit 8g in the GitHub repository.)

Email address changes

Users can be given the option to change the registered email address, but before the new address is accepted it must be verified with a confirmation email. To use this feature, the user enters the new email address in a form. To confirm the email address, a token is emailed to that address. When the server receives the token back, it can update the user object. While the server waits to receive the token, it can store the new email address in a new database field reserved for pending email addresses, or it can store the address in the token along with the id. (This feature is implemented as commit 8h in the GitHub repository.)

In the next chapter, the user subsystem of Flasky will be extended through the use of user roles.

## CHAPTER 9

User Roles

Not all users of web applications are created equal. In most applications, a small percentage of users are trusted with extra powers to help keep the application running smoothly. Administrators are the best example, but in many cases middle-level power users such as content moderators exist as well.

There are several ways to implement roles in an application. The appropriate method largely depends on how many roles need to be supported and how elaborate they are. For example, a simple application may need just two roles, one for regular users and one for administrators. In this case, having an `is_administrator` Boolean field in the `User` model may be all that is necessary. A more complex application may need additional roles with varying levels of power in between regular users and administrators. In some applications it may not even make sense to talk about discrete roles; instead, giving users a combination of *permissions* may be the right approach.

The user role implementation presented in this chapter is a hybrid between discrete roles and permissions. Users are assigned a discrete role, but the roles are defined in terms of permissions.

Database Representation of Roles

A simple `roles` table was created in Chapter 5 as a vehicle to demonstrate one-to-many relationships. Example 9-1 shows an improved `Role` model with some additions.

Example 9-1. app/models.py: Role permissions

```
class Role(db.Model):
    __tablename__ = 'roles'
    id = db.Column(db.Integer, primary_key=True)
    name = db.Column(db.String(64), unique=True)
    default = db.Column(db.Boolean, default=False, index=True)
```

```
permissions = db.Column(db.Integer)
users = db.relationship('User', backref='role', lazy='dynamic')
```

The `default` field should be set to `True` for only one role and `False` for all the others. The role marked as default will be the one assigned to new users upon registration.

The second addition to the model is the `permissions` field, which is an integer that will be used as bit flags. Each task will be assigned a bit position, and for each role the tasks that are allowed for that role will have their bits set to 1.

The list of tasks for which permissions are needed is obviously application specific. For Flasky, the list of tasks is shown in Table 9-1.

Table 9-1. Application permissions

Task name	Bit value	Description
Follow users	0b00000001 (0x01)	Follow other users
Comment on posts made by others	0b00000010 (0x02)	Comment on articles written by others
Write articles	0b00000100 (0x04)	Write original articles
Moderate comments made by others	0b00001000 (0x08)	Suppress offensive comments made by others
Administration access	0b10000000 (0x80)	Administrative access to the site

Note that a total of eight bits was allocated to tasks, and so far only five have been used. The remaining three are left for future expansion.

The code representation of Table 9-1 is shown in Example 9-2.

Example 9-2. app/models.py: Permission constants

```
class Permission:
    FOLLOW = 0x01
    COMMENT = 0x02
    WRITE_ARTICLES = 0x04
    MODERATE_COMMENTS = 0x08
    ADMINISTER = 0x80
```

Table 9-2 shows the list of user roles that will be supported, along with the permission bits that define it.

Table 9-2. User roles

User role	Permissions	Description
Anonymous	0b00000000 (0x00)	User who is not logged in. Read-only access to the application.
User	0b00000111 (0x07)	Basic permissions to write articles and comments and to follow other users. This is the default for new users.
Moderator	0b00001111 (0x0f)	Adds permission to suppress comments deemed offensive or inappropriate.
Administrator	0b11111111 (0xff)	Full access, which includes permission to change the roles of other users.

Organizing the roles with permissions lets you add new roles in the future that use different combinations of permissions.

Adding the roles to the database manually is time consuming and error prone. Instead, a class method will be added to the `Role` class for this purpose, as shown in Example 9-3.

Example 9-3. app/models.py: Create roles in the database

```python
class Role(db.Model):
    # ...
    @staticmethod
    def insert_roles():
        roles = {
            'User': (Permission.FOLLOW |
                     Permission.COMMENT |
                     Permission.WRITE_ARTICLES, True),
            'Moderator': (Permission.FOLLOW |
                          Permission.COMMENT |
                          Permission.WRITE_ARTICLES |
                          Permission.MODERATE_COMMENTS, False),
            'Administrator': (0xff, False)
        }
        for r in roles:
            role = Role.query.filter_by(name=r).first()
            if role is None:
                role = Role(name=r)
            role.permissions = roles[r][0]
            role.default = roles[r][1]
            db.session.add(role)
        db.session.commit()
```

The `insert_roles()` function does not directly create new role objects. Instead, it tries to find existing roles by name and update those. A new role object is created only for role names that aren't in the database already. This is done so that the role list can be updated in the future when changes need to be made. To add a new role or change the permission assignments for a role, change the `roles` array and rerun the function. Note that the "Anonymous" role does not need to be represented in the database, as it is designed to represent users who are not in the database.

To apply these roles to the database, a shell session can be used:

```
(venv) $ python manage.py shell
>>> Role.insert_roles()
>>> Role.query.all()
[<Role u'Administrator'>, <Role u'User'>, <Role u'Moderator'>]
```

Role Assignment

When users register an account with the application, the correct role should be assigned to them. For most users, the role assigned at registration time will be the "User" role, as that is the role that is marked as a default role. The only exception is made for the administrator, which needs to be assigned the "Administrator" role from the start. This user is identified by an email address stored in the FLASKY_ADMIN configuration variable, so as soon as that email address appears in a registration request it can be given the correct role. Example 9-4 shows how this is done in the User model constructor.

Example 9-4. app/models.py: Define a default role for users

```python
class User(UserMixin, db.Model):
    # ...
    def __init__(self, **kwargs):
        super(User, self).__init__(**kwargs)
        if self.role is None:
            if self.email == current_app.config['FLASKY_ADMIN']:
                self.role = Role.query.filter_by(permissions=0xff).first()
            if self.role is None:
                self.role = Role.query.filter_by(default=True).first()
    # ...
```

The User constructor first invokes the constructors of the base classes, and if after that the object does not have a role defined, it sets the administrator or default roles depending on the email address.

Role Verification

To simplify the implementation of roles and permissions, a helper method can be added to the User model that checks whether a given permission is present, as shown in Example 9-5.

Example 9-5. app/models.py: Evaluate whether a user has a given permission

```python
from flask.ext.login import UserMixin, AnonymousUserMixin

class User(UserMixin, db.Model):
    # ...

    def can(self, permissions):
        return self.role is not None and \
            (self.role.permissions & permissions) == permissions

    def is_administrator(self):
        return self.can(Permission.ADMINISTER)

class AnonymousUser(AnonymousUserMixin):
    def can(self, permissions):
        return False

    def is_administrator(self):
        return False
```

```
login_manager.anonymous_user = AnonymousUser
```

The can() method added to the User model performs a *bitwise and* operation between the requested permissions and the permissions of the assigned role. The method returns True if all the requested bits are present in the role, which means that the user should be allowed to perform the task. The check for administration permissions is so common that it is also implemented as a standalone is_administrator() method.

For consistency, a custom AnonymousUser class that implements the can() and is_administrator() methods is created. This object inherits from Flask-Login's AnonymousUserMixin class and is registered as the class of the object that is assigned to current_user when the user is not logged in. This will enable the application to freely call current_user.can() and current_user.is_administrator() without having to check whether the user is logged in first.

For cases in which an entire view function needs to be made available only to users with certain permissions, a custom decorator can be used. Example 9-6 shows the implementation of two decorators, one for generic permission checks and one that checks specifically for administrator permission.

Example 9-6. app/decorators.py: Custom decorators that check user permissions
```
from functools import wraps
from flask import abort
from flask.ext.login import current_user

def permission_required(permission):
    def decorator(f):
        @wraps(f)
        def decorated_function(*args, **kwargs):
            if not current_user.can(permission):
                abort(403)
            return f(*args, **kwargs)
        return decorated_function
    return decorator

def admin_required(f):
    return permission_required(Permission.ADMINISTER)(f)
```

These decorators are built with the help of the *functools* package from the Python standard library, and return an error code 403, the "Forbidden" HTTP error, when the current user does not have the requested permissions. In Chapter 3, custom error pages were created for errors 404 and 500, so now a page for the 403 error needs to be added as well.

The following are two examples that demonstrate the usage of these decorators:

```
from decorators import admin_required, permission_required

@main.route('/admin')
@login_required
@admin_required
def for_admins_only():
    return "For administrators!"

@main.route('/moderator')
@login_required
@permission_required(Permission.MODERATE_COMMENTS)
def for_moderators_only():
    return "For comment moderators!"
```

Permissions may also need to be checked from templates, so the Permission class with all the bit constants needs to be accessible to them. To avoid having to add a template argument in every render_template() call, a *context processor* can be used. Context processors make variables globally available to all templates. This change is shown in Example 9-7.

Example 9-7. app/main/__init__.py: Adding the Permission class to the template context

```
@main.app_context_processor
def inject_permissions():
    return dict(Permission=Permission)
```

The new roles and permissions can be exercised in unit tests. Example 9-8 shows two simple tests that also serve as a demonstration of the usage.

Example 9-8. tests/test_user_model.py: Unit tests for roles and permissions

```
class UserModelTestCase(unittest.TestCase):
    # ...

    def test_roles_and_permissions(self):
        Role.insert_roles()
        u = User(email='john@example.com', password='cat')
        self.assertTrue(u.can(Permission.WRITE_ARTICLES))
        self.assertFalse(u.can(Permission.MODERATE_COMMENTS))

    def test_anonymous_user(self):
        u = AnonymousUser()
        self.assertFalse(u.can(Permission.FOLLOW))
```

 If you have cloned the application's Git repository on GitHub, you can run git checkout 9a to check out this version of the application. This update contains a database migration, so remember to run python manage.py db upgrade after you check out the code.

Before you move to the next chapter, it is a good idea to re-create or update the development database so that all the user accounts that were created before roles and permissions existed have a role assigned.

The user system is now fairly complete. The next chapter will make use of it to create user profile pages.

## CHAPTER 10

User Profiles

In this chapter, user profiles for Flasky are implemented. All socially aware sites give their users a profile page, where a summary of the user's participation in the website is presented. Users can advertise their presence on the website by sharing the URL to their profile page, so it is important that the URLs be short and easy to remember.

Profile Information

To make user profile pages more interesting, some additional information about users can be recorded. In Example 10-1 the User model is extended with several new fields.

Example 10-1. app/models.py: User information fields

```
class User(UserMixin, db.Model):
    # ...
    name = db.Column(db.String(64))
    location = db.Column(db.String(64))
    about_me = db.Column(db.Text())
    member_since = db.Column(db.DateTime(), default=datetime.utcnow)
    last_seen = db.Column(db.DateTime(), default=datetime.utcnow)
```

The new fields store the user's real name, location, self-written description, date of registration, and date of last visit. The about_me field is assigned the type db.Text(). The difference between db.String and db.Text is that db.Text does not need a maximum length.

The two timestamps are given a default value of the current time. Note that datetime.utcnow is missing the () at the end. This is because the default argument to db.Column() can take a function as a default value, so each time a default value needs to be generated the function is invoked to produce it. This default value is all that is needed to manage the member_since field.

The `last_seen` field is also initialized to the current time upon creation, but it needs to be refreshed each time the user accesses the site. A method in the `User` class can be added to perform this update. This is shown in Example 10-2.

Example 10-2. app/models.py: Refresh last visit time of a user

```
class User(UserMixin, db.Model):
    # ...

    def ping(self):
        self.last_seen = datetime.utcnow()
        db.session.add(self)
```

The `ping()` method must be called each time a request from the user is received. Because the `before_app_request` handler in the `auth` blueprint runs before every request, it can do this easily, as shown in Example 10-3.

Example 10-3. app/auth/views.py: Ping logged-in user

```
@auth.before_app_request
def before_request():
    if current_user.is_authenticated():
        current_user.ping()
        if not current_user.confirmed \
                and request.endpoint[:5] != 'auth.':
            return redirect(url_for('auth.unconfirmed'))
```

User Profile Page

Creating a profile page for each user does not present any new challenges. Example 10-4 shows the route definition.

Example 10-4. app/main/views.py: Profile page route

```
@main.route('/user/<username>')
def user(username):
    user = User.query.filter_by(username=username).first()
    if user is None:
        abort(404)
    return render_template('user.html', user=user)
```

This route is added in the `main` blueprint. For a user named `john`, the profile page will be at *http://localhost:5000/user/john*. The username given in the URL is searched in the database and, if found, the *user.html* template is rendered with it as the argument. An invalid username sent into this route will cause a 404 error to be returned. The *user.html* template should render the information stored in the user object. An initial version of this template is shown in Example 10-5.

Example 10-5. app/templates/user.html: User profile template

```
{% block page_content %}
<div class="page-header">
    <h1>{{ user.username }}</h1>
    {% if user.name or user.location %}
    <p>
        {% if user.name %}{{ user.name }}{% endif %}
        {% if user.location %}
            From <a href="http://maps.google.com/?q={{ user.location }}">
                {{ user.location }}
            </a>
        {% endif %}
    </p>
    {% endif %}
    {% if current_user.is_administrator() %}
    <p><a href="mailto:{{ user.email }}">{{ user.email }}</a></p>
    {% endif %}
    {% if user.about_me %}<p>{{ user.about_me }}</p>{% endif %}
    <p>
        Member since {{ moment(user.member_since).format('L') }}.
        Last seen {{ moment(user.last_seen).fromNow() }}.
    </p>
</div>
{% endblock %}
```

This template has a few interesting implementation details:

- The `name` and `location` fields are rendered inside a single <p> element. Only when at least one of the fields is defined is the <p> element created.

- The user `location` field is rendered as a link to a Google Maps query.

- If the logged-in user is an administrator, then email addresses are shown, rendered as a *mailto* link.

As most users will want easy access to their own profile page, a link to it can be added to the navigation bar. The relevant changes to the *base.html* template are shown in Example 10-6.

Example 10-6. app/templates/base.html

```
{% if current_user.is_authenticated() %}
<li>
    <a href="{{ url_for('main.user', username=current_user.username) }}">
        Profile
    </a>
</li>
{% endif %}
```

Using a conditional for the profile page link is necessary because the navigation bar is also rendered for nonauthenticated users, in which case the profile link is skipped.

Figure 10-1 shows how the profile page looks in the browser. The new profile link in the navigation bar is also shown.

If you have cloned the application's Git repository on GitHub, you can run `git checkout 10a` to check out this version of the application. This update contains a database migration, so remember to run `python manage.py db upgrade` after you check out the code.

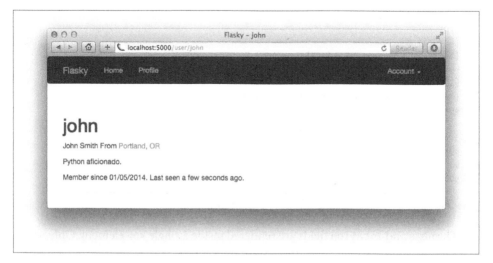

Figure 10-1. User profile page

Profile Editor

There are two different use cases related to editing of user profiles. The most obvious is that users need to have access to a page where they can enter information about themselves to present in their profile pages. A less obvious but also important requirement is to let administrators edit the profile of any users—not only the personal information items but also other fields in the User model to which users have no direct access, such as the user role. Because the two profile editing requirements are substantially different, two different forms will be created.

User-Level Profile Editor

The profile edit form for regular users is shown in Example 10-7.

Example 10-7. app/main/forms.py: Profile edit form

```python
class EditProfileForm(Form):
    name = StringField('Real name', validators=[Length(0, 64)])
    location = StringField('Location', validators=[Length(0, 64)])
    about_me = TextAreaField('About me')
    submit = SubmitField('Submit')
```

Note that as all the fields in this form are optional, the length validator allows a length of zero. The route definition that uses this form is shown in Example 10-8.

Example 10-8. app/main/views.py: Profile edit route

```python
@main.route('/edit-profile', methods=['GET', 'POST'])
@login_required
def edit_profile():
    form = EditProfileForm()
    if form.validate_on_submit():
        current_user.name = form.name.data
        current_user.location = form.location.data
        current_user.about_me = form.about_me.data
        db.session.add(user)
        flash('Your profile has been updated.')
        return redirect(url_for('.user', username=current_user.username))
    form.name.data = current_user.name
    form.location.data = current_user.location
    form.about_me.data = current_user.about_me
    return render_template('edit_profile.html', form=form)
```

This view function sets initial values for all the fields before presenting the form. For any given field, this is done by assigning the initial value to `form.<field-name>.data`. When `form.validate_on_submit()` is `False`, the three fields in this form are initialized from the corresponding fields in `current_user`. Then, when the form is submitted, the `data` attributes of the form fields contain the updated values, so these are moved back into the fields of the user object and the object is added to the database session. Figure 10-2 shows the Edit Profile page.

To make it easy for users to reach this page, a direct link can be added in the profile page, as shown in Example 10-9.

Example 10-9. app/templates/user.html: Profile edit link

```html
{% if user == current_user %}
<a class="btn btn-default" href="{{ url_for('.edit_profile') }}">
    Edit Profile
</a>
{% endif %}
```

The conditional that encloses the link will make the link appear only when users are viewing their own profiles.

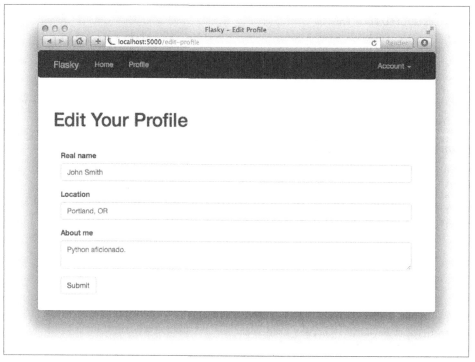

Figure 10-2. Profile editor

Administrator-Level Profile Editor

The profile edit form for administrators is more complex than the one for regular users. In addition to the three profile information fields, this form allows administrators to edit a user's email, username, confirmed status, and role. The form is shown in Example 10-10.

Example 10-10. app/main/forms.py: Profile editing form for administrators

```
class EditProfileAdminForm(Form):
    email = StringField('Email', validators=[Required(), Length(1, 64),
                                              Email()])
    username = StringField('Username', validators=[
        Required(), Length(1, 64), Regexp('^[A-Za-z][A-Za-z0-9_.]*$', 0,
                                          'Usernames must have only letters, '
                                          'numbers, dots or underscores')])
    confirmed = BooleanField('Confirmed')
    role = SelectField('Role', coerce=int)
    name = StringField('Real name', validators=[Length(0, 64)])
    location = StringField('Location', validators=[Length(0, 64)])
    about_me = TextAreaField('About me')
    submit = SubmitField('Submit')
```

```
def __init__(self, user, *args, **kwargs):
    super(EditProfileAdminForm, self).__init__(*args, **kwargs)
    self.role.choices = [(role.id, role.name)
                         for role in Role.query.order_by(Role.name).all()]
    self.user = user

def validate_email(self, field):
    if field.data != self.user.email and \
            User.query.filter_by(email=field.data).first():
        raise ValidationError('Email already registered.')

def validate_username(self, field):
    if field.data != self.user.username and \
            User.query.filter_by(username=field.data).first():
        raise ValidationError('Username already in use.')
```

The SelectField is WTForm's wrapper for the <select> HTML form control, which implements a dropdown list, used in this form to select a user role. An instance of SelectField must have the items set in its choices attribute. They must be given as a list of tuples, with each tuple consisting of two values: an identifier for the item and the text to show in the control as a string. The choices list is set in the form's constructor, with values obtained from the Role model with a query that sorts all the roles alphabetically by name. The identifier for each tuple is set to the id of each role, and since these are integers, a coerce=int argument is added to the SelectField constructor so that the field values are stored as integers instead of the default, which is strings.

The email and username fields are constructed in the same way as in the authentication forms, but their validation requires some careful handling. The validation condition used for both these fields must first check whether a change to the field was made, and only when there is a change should it ensure that the new value does not duplicate another user's. When these fields are not changed, then validation should pass. To implement this logic, the form's constructor receives the user object as an argument and saves it as a member variable, which is later used in the custom validation methods.

The route definition for the administrator's profile editor is shown in Example 10-11.

Example 10-11. app/main/views.py: Profile edit route for administrators

```
@main.route('/edit-profile/<int:id>', methods=['GET', 'POST'])
@login_required
@admin_required
def edit_profile_admin(id):
    user = User.query.get_or_404(id)
    form = EditProfileAdminForm(user=user)
    if form.validate_on_submit():
        user.email = form.email.data
        user.username = form.username.data
        user.confirmed = form.confirmed.data
```

```
            user.role = Role.query.get(form.role.data)
            user.name = form.name.data
            user.location = form.location.data
            user.about_me = form.about_me.data
            db.session.add(user)
            flash('The profile has been updated.')
            return redirect(url_for('.user', username=user.username))
        form.email.data = user.email
        form.username.data = user.username
        form.confirmed.data = user.confirmed
        form.role.data = user.role_id
        form.name.data = user.name
        form.location.data = user.location
        form.about_me.data = user.about_me
        return render_template('edit_profile.html', form=form, user=user)
```

This route has largely the same structure as the simpler one for regular users. In this view function, the user is given by its id, so Flask-SQLAlchemy's get_or_404() convenience function can be used, knowing that if the id is invalid the request will return a code 404 error.

The SelectField used for the user role also deserves to be studied. When setting the initial value for the field, the role_id is assigned to field.role.data because the list of tuples set in the choices attribute uses the numeric identifiers to reference each option. When the form is submitted, the id is extracted from the field's data attribute and used in a query to load the role object by its id. The coerce=int argument used in the SelectField declaration in the form ensures that the data attribute of this field is an integer.

To link to this page, another button is added in the user profile page, as shown in Example 10-12.

Example 10-12. app/templates/user.html: Profile edit link for administrator

```
{% if current_user.is_administrator() %}
<a class="btn btn-danger"
        href="{{ url_for('.edit_profile_admin', id=user.id) }}">
    Edit Profile [Admin]
</a>
{% endif %}
```

This button is rendered with a different Bootstrap style to call attention to it. The conditional in this case makes the button appear in profile pages if the logged-in user is an administrator.

If you have cloned the application's Git repository on GitHub, you can run git checkout 10b to check out this version of the application.

User Avatars

The look of the profile pages can be improved by showing avatar pictures of users. In this section, you will learn how to add user avatars provided by Gravatar (*http://gravatar.com/*), the leading avatar service. Gravatar associates avatar images with email addresses. Users create an account at *http://gravatar.com* and then upload their images. To generate the avatar URL for a given email address, its MD5 hash is calculated:

```
(venv) $ python
>>> import hashlib
>>> hashlib.md5('john@example.com'.encode('utf-8')).hexdigest()
'd4c74594d841139328695756648b6bd6'
```

The avatar URLs are then generated by appending the MD5 hash to URL *http://www.gravatar.com/avatar/* or *https://secure.gravatar.com/avatar/*. For example, you can type *http://www.gravatar.com/avatar/d4c74594d841139328695756648b6bd6* in your browser's address bar to get the avatar image for the email address john@example.com, or a default generated image if that email address does not have an avatar registered. The query string of the URL can include several arguments that configure the characteristics of the avatar image, listed in Table 10-1.

Table 10-1. Gravatar query string arguments

Argument name	Description
s	Image size, in pixels.
r	Image rating. Options are `"g"`, `"pg"`, `"r"`, and `"x"`.
d	The default image generator for users who have no avatars registered with the Gravatar service. Options are `"404"` to return a 404 error, a URL that points to a default image, or one of the following image generators: `"mm"`, `"identicon"`, `"monsterid"`, `"wavatar"`, `"retro"`, or `"blank"`.
fd	Force the use of default avatars.

The knowledge of how to build a Gravatar URL can be added to the User model. The implementation is shown in Example 10-13.

Example 10-13. app/models.py: Gravatar URL generation

```
import hashlib
from flask import request

class User(UserMixin, db.Model):
```

```
# ...
def gravatar(self, size=100, default='identicon', rating='g'):
    if request.is_secure:
        url = 'https://secure.gravatar.com/avatar'
    else:
        url = 'http://www.gravatar.com/avatar'
    hash = hashlib.md5(self.email.encode('utf-8')).hexdigest()
    return '{url}/{hash}?s={size}&d={default}&r={rating}'.format(
        url=url, hash=hash, size=size, default=default, rating=rating)
```

This implementation selects the standard or secure Gravatar base URL to match the security of the client request. The avatar URL is generated from the base URL, the MD5 hash of the user's email address, and the arguments, all of which have default values. With this implementation it is easy to generate avatar URLs in the Python shell:

```
(venv) $ python manage.py shell
>>> u = User(email='john@example.com')
>>> u.gravatar()
'http://www.gravatar.com/avatar/d4c74594d84113932869575bd6?s=100&d=identicon&r=g'
>>> u.gravatar(size=256)
'http://www.gravatar.com/avatar/d4c74594d84113932869575bd6?s=256&d=identicon&r=g'
```

The gravatar() method can also be invoked from Jinja2 templates. Example 10-14 shows how a 256-pixel avatar can be added to the profile page.

Example 10-14. app/tempaltes/user.html: Avatar in profile page

```
...
<img class="img-rounded profile-thumbnail" src="{{ user.gravatar(size=256) }}">
...
```

Using a similar approach, the base template adds a small thumbnail image of the logged-in user in the navigation bar. To better format the avatar pictures in the page, custom CSS classes are used. You can find these in the source code repository in a *styles.css* file added to the application's static file folder and referenced from the *base.html* template. Figure 10-3 shows the user profile page with avatar.

 If you have cloned the application's Git repository on GitHub, you can run git checkout 10c to check out this version of the application.

The generation of avatars requires an MD5 hash to be generated, which is a CPU-intensive operation. If a large number of avatars need to be generated for a page, then the computational work can be significant. Since the MD5 hash for a user will remain constant, it can be *cached* in the User model. Example 10-15 shows the changes to the User model to store the MD5 hashes in the database.

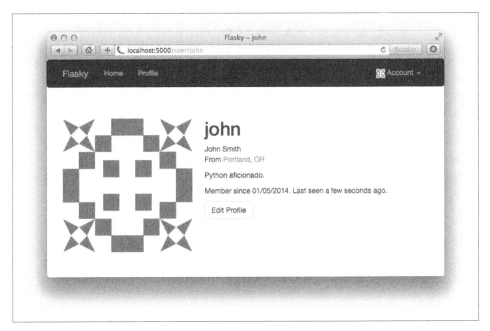

Figure 10-3. User profile page with avatar

Example 10-15. app/models.py: Gravatar URL generation with caching of MD5 hashes

```python
class User(UserMixin, db.Model):
    # ...
    avatar_hash = db.Column(db.String(32))

    def __init__(self, **kwargs):
        # ...
        if self.email is not None and self.avatar_hash is None:
            self.avatar_hash = hashlib.md5(
                self.email.encode('utf-8')).hexdigest()

    def change_email(self, token):
        # ...
        self.email = new_email
        self.avatar_hash = hashlib.md5(
            self.email.encode('utf-8')).hexdigest()
        db.session.add(self)
        return True

    def gravatar(self, size=100, default='identicon', rating='g'):
        if request.is_secure:
            url = 'https://secure.gravatar.com/avatar'
        else:
            url = 'http://www.gravatar.com/avatar'
        hash = self.avatar_hash or hashlib.md5(
```

```
        self.email.encode('utf-8')).hexdigest()
    return '{url}/{hash}?s={size}&d={default}&r={rating}'.format(
        url=url, hash=hash, size=size, default=default, rating=rating)
```

During model initialization, the hash is calculated from the email and stored, and in the event that the user updates the email address the hash is recalculated. The `gravatar()` method uses the hash from the model if available; if not, it works as before and generates the hash from the email address.

 If you have cloned the application's Git repository on GitHub, you can run `git checkout 10d` to check out this version of the application. This update contains a database migration, so remember to run `python manage.py db upgrade` after you check out the code.

In the next chapter, the blogging engine that powers this application will be created.

## CHAPTER 11

Blog Posts

This chapter is dedicated to the implementation of Flasky's main feature, which is to allow users to read and write blog posts. Here you will learn a few new techniques for reuse of templates, pagination of long lists of items, and working with rich text.

Blog Post Submission and Display

To support blog posts, a new database model that represents them is necessary. This model is shown in Example 11-1.

Example 11-1. app/models.py: Post model

```python
class Post(db.Model):
    __tablename__ = 'posts'
    id = db.Column(db.Integer, primary_key=True)
    body = db.Column(db.Text)
    timestamp = db.Column(db.DateTime, index=True, default=datetime.utcnow)
    author_id = db.Column(db.Integer, db.ForeignKey('users.id'))

class User(UserMixin, db.Model):
    # ...
    posts = db.relationship('Post', backref='author', lazy='dynamic')
```

A blog post is is represented by a body, a timestamp, and a one-to-many relationship from the User model. The body field is defined with type db.Text so that there is no limitation on the length.

The form that will be shown in the main page of the application lets users write a blog post. This form is very simple; it contains just a text area where the blog post can be typed and a submit button. The form definition is shown in Example 11-2.

Example 11-2. app/main/forms.py: Blog post form

```
class PostForm(Form):
    body = TextAreaField("What's on your mind?", validators=[Required()])
    submit = SubmitField('Submit')
```

The index() view function handles the form and passes the list of old blog posts to the template, as shown in Example 11-3.

Example 11-3. app/main/views.py: Home page route with a blog post

```
@main.route('/', methods=['GET', 'POST'])
def index():
    form = PostForm()
    if current_user.can(Permission.WRITE_ARTICLES) and \
            form.validate_on_submit():
        post = Post(body=form.body.data,
                    author=current_user._get_current_object())
        db.session.add(post)
        return redirect(url_for('.index'))
    posts = Post.query.order_by(Post.timestamp.desc()).all()
    return render_template('index.html', form=form, posts=posts)
```

This view function passes the form and the complete list of blog posts to the template. The list of posts is ordered by their timestamp in descending order. The blog post form is handled in the usual manner, with the creation of a new Post instance when a valid submission is received. The current user's permission to write articles is checked before allowing the new post.

Note the way the author attribute of the new post object is set to the expression current_user._get_current_object(). The current_user variable from Flask-Login, like all context variables, is implemented as a thread-local proxy object. This object behaves like a user object but is really a thin wrapper that contains the actual user object inside. The database needs a real user object, which is obtained by calling _get_current_object().

The form is rendered below the greeting in the *index.html* template, followed by the blog posts. The list of blog posts is a first attempt to create a blog post timeline, with all the blog posts in the database listed in chronological order from newest to oldest. The changes to the template are shown in Example 11-4.

Example 11-4. app/templates/index.html: Home page template with blog posts

```
{% extends "base.html" %}
{% import "bootstrap/wtf.html" as wtf %}
...
<div>
    {% if current_user.can(Permission.WRITE_ARTICLES) %}
    {{ wtf.quick_form(form) }}
    {% endif %}
```

```
</div>
<ul class="posts">
    {% for post in posts %}
    <li class="post">
        <div class="profile-thumbnail">
            <a href="{{ url_for('.user', username=post.author.username) }}">
                <img class="img-rounded profile-thumbnail"
                    src="{{ post.author.gravatar(size=40) }}">
            </a>
        </div>
        <div class="post-date">{{ moment(post.timestamp).fromNow() }}</div>
        <div class="post-author">
            <a href="{{ url_for('.user', username=post.author.username) }}">
                {{ post.author.username }}
            </a>
        </div>
        <div class="post-body">{{ post.body }}</div>
    </li>
    {% endfor %}
</ul>
...
```

Note that the `User.can()` method is used to skip the blog post form for users who do
not have the `WRITE_ARTICLES` permission in their role. The blog post list is implemented
as an HTML unordered list, with CSS classes giving it nicer formatting. A small avatar
of the author is rendered on the left side, and both the avatar and the author's username
are rendered as links to the user profile page. The CSS styles used are stored in a *styles.css*
file in the application's *static* folder. You can review this file in the GitHub repository.
Figure 11-1 shows the home page with submission form and blog post list.

> If you have cloned the application's Git repository on GitHub, you can
> run `git checkout 11a` to check out this version of the application.
> This update contains a database migration, so remember to run
> `python manage.py db upgrade` after you check out the code.

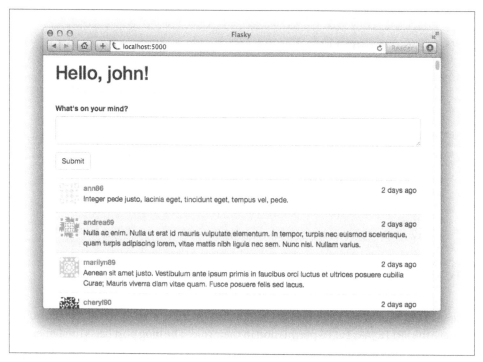

Figure 11-1. Home page with blog submission form and blog post list

Blog Posts on Profile Pages

The user profile page can be improved by showing a list of blog posts authored by the user. Example 11-5 shows the changes to the view function to obtain the post list.

Example 11-5. app/main/views.py: Profile page route with blog posts

```
@main.route('/user/<username>')
def user(username):
    user = User.query.filter_by(username=username).first()
    if user is None:
        abort(404)
    posts = user.posts.order_by(Post.timestamp.desc()).all()
    return render_template('user.html', user=user, posts=posts)
```

The list of blog posts for a user is obtained from the User.posts relationship, which is a query object, so filters such as order_by() can be used on it as well.

The *user.html* template requires the <ul> HTML tree that renders a list of blog posts like the one in *index.html*. Having to maintain two identical copies of a piece of HTML is not ideal, so for cases like this, Jinja2's include() directive is very useful. The *user.html* template includes the list from an external file, as shown in Example 11-6.

Example 11-6. app/templates/user.html: Profile page template with blog posts

```
...
<h3>Posts by {{ user.username }}</h3>
{% include '_posts.html' %}
...
```

To complete this reorganization, the `<ul>` tree from *index.html* is moved to the new template *_posts.html*, and replaced with another `include()` directive. Note that the use of an underscore prefix in the *_posts.html* template name is not a requirement; this is merely a convention to distinguish standalone and partial templates.

 If you have cloned the application's Git repository on GitHub, you can run `git checkout 11b` to check out this version of the application.

Paginating Long Blog Post Lists

As the site grows and the number of blog posts increases, it will become slow and impractical to show the complete list of posts on the home and profile pages. Big pages take longer to generate, download, and render in the web browser, so the quality of the user experience decreases as the pages get larger. The solution is to *paginate* the data and render it in chunks.

Creating Fake Blog Post Data

To be able to work with multiple pages of blog posts, it is necessary to have a test database with a large volume of data. Manually adding new database entries is time consuming and tedious; an automated solution is more appropriate. There are several Python packages that can be used to generate fake information. A fairly complete one is *ForgeryPy*, which is installed with pip:

```
(venv) $ pip install forgerypy
```

The ForgeryPy package is not, strictly speaking, a dependency of the application, because it is needed only during development. To separate the production dependencies from the development dependencies, the *requirements.txt* file can be replaced with a *requirements* folder that stores different sets of dependencies. Inside this new folder a *dev.txt* file can list the dependencies that are necessary for development and a *prod.txt* file can list the dependencies that are needed in production. As there is a large number of dependencies that will be in both lists, a *common.txt* file is added for those, and then the *dev.txt* and *prod.txt* lists use the `-r` prefix to include it. Example 11-7 shows the *dev.txt* file.

Example 11-7. requirements/dev.txt: Development requirements file

```
-r common.txt
ForgeryPy==0.1
```

Example 11-8 shows class methods added to the User and Post models that can generate fake data.

Example 11-8. app/models.py: Generate fake users and blog posts

```python
class User(UserMixin, db.Model):
    # ...
    @staticmethod
    def generate_fake(count=100):
        from sqlalchemy.exc import IntegrityError
        from random import seed
        import forgery_py

        seed()
        for i in range(count):
            u = User(email=forgery_py.internet.email_address(),
                     username=forgery_py.internet.user_name(True),
                     password=forgery_py.lorem_ipsum.word(),
                     confirmed=True,
                     name=forgery_py.name.full_name(),
                     location=forgery_py.address.city(),
                     about_me=forgery_py.lorem_ipsum.sentence(),
                     member_since=forgery_py.date.date(True))
            db.session.add(u)
            try:
                db.session.commit()
            except IntegrityError:
                db.session.rollback()

class Post(db.Model):
    # ...
    @staticmethod
    def generate_fake(count=100):
        from random import seed, randint
        import forgery_py

        seed()
        user_count = User.query.count()
        for i in range(count):
            u = User.query.offset(randint(0, user_count - 1)).first()
            p = Post(body=forgery_py.lorem_ipsum.sentences(randint(1, 3)),
                     timestamp=forgery_py.date.date(True),
                     author=u)
            db.session.add(p)
            db.session.commit()
```

The attributes of these fake objects are generated with ForgeryPy random information generators, which can generate real-looking names, emails, sentences, and many more attributes.

The email addresses and usernames of users must be unique, but since ForgeryPy generates these in completely random fashion, there is a risk of having duplicates. In this unlikely event, the database session commit will throw an `IntegrityError` exception. This exception is handled by rolling back the session before continuing. The loop iterations that produce a duplicate will not write a user to the database, so the total number of fake users added can be less than the number requested.

The random post generation must assign a random user to each post. For this the `offset()` query filter is used. This filter discards the number of results given as an argument. By setting a random offset and then calling `first()`, a different random user is obtained each time.

 If you have cloned the application's Git repository on GitHub, you can run `git checkout 11c` to check out this version of the application. To ensure that you have all the dependencies installed, also run `pip install -r requirements/dev.txt`.

The new methods make it easy to create a large number of fake users and posts from the Python shell:

```
(venv) $ python manage.py shell
>>> User.generate_fake(100)
>>> Post.generate_fake(100)
```

If you run the application now, you will see a long list of random blog posts on the home page.

Rendering Data on Pages

Example 11-9 shows the changes to the home page route to support pagination.

Example 11-9. app/main/views.py: Paginate the blog post list

```
@main.route('/', methods=['GET', 'POST'])
def index():
    # ...
    page = request.args.get('page', 1, type=int)
    pagination = Post.query.order_by(Post.timestamp.desc()).paginate(
        page, per_page=current_app.config['FLASKY_POSTS_PER_PAGE'],
        error_out=False)
    posts = pagination.items
    return render_template('index.html', form=form, posts=posts,
                           pagination=pagination)
```

The page number to render is obtained from the request's query string, which is available as `request.args`. When an explicit page isn't given, a default page of 1 (the first page) is used. The `type=int` argument ensures that if the argument cannot be converted to an integer, the default value is returned.

To load a single page of records, the call to `all()` is replaced with Flask-SQLAlchemy's `paginate()`. The `paginate()` method takes the page number as the first and only required argument. An optional `per_page` argument can be given to indicate the size of each page, in number of items. If this argument is not specified, the default is 20 items per page. Another optional argument called `error_out` can be set to `True` (the default) to issue a code 404 error when a page outside of the valid range is requested. If `error_out` is `False`, pages outside of the valid range are returned with an empty list of items. To make the page sizes configurable, the value of the `per_page` argument is read from an application-specific configuration variable called `FLASKY_POSTS_PER_PAGE`.

With these changes, the blog post list in the home page will show a limited number of items. To see the second page of posts, add a *?page=2* query string to the URL in the browser's address bar.

Adding a Pagination Widget

The return value of `paginate()` is an object of class `Pagination`, a class defined by Flask-SQLAlchemy. This object contains several properties that are useful to generate page links in a template, so it is passed to the template as an argument. A summary of the attributes of the pagination object is shown in Table 11-1.

Table 11-1. Flask-SQLAlchemy pagination object attributes

Attribute	Description
items	The records in the current page
query	The source query that was paginated
page	The current page number
prev_num	The previous page number
next_num	The next page number
has_next	True if there is a next page
has_prev	True if there is a previous page
pages	The total number of pages for the query
per_page	The number of items per page
total	The total number of items returned by the query

The pagination object also has some methods, listed in Table 11-2.

Table 11-2. Flask-SQLAlchemy pagination object attributes

Method	Description
`iter_pages(left_edge=2, left_current=2, right_current=5, right_edge=2)`	An iterator that returns the sequence of page numbers to display in a pagination widget. The list will have `left_edge` pages on the left side, `left_current` pages to the left of the current page, `right_current` pages to the right of the current page, and `right_edge` pages on the right side. For example, for page 50 of 100 this iterator configured with default values will return the following pages: 1, 2, None, 48, 49, 50, 51, 52, 53, 54, 55, None, 99, 100. A None value in the sequence indicates a gap in the sequence of pages.
`prev()`	A pagination object for the previous page.
`next()`	A pagination object for the next page.

Armed with this powerful object and Bootstrap's pagination CSS classes, it is quite easy to build a pagination footer in the template. The implementation shown in Example 11-10 is done as a reusable Jinja2 macro.

Example 11-10. app/templates/_macros.html: Pagination template macro

```
{% macro pagination_widget(pagination, endpoint) %}
<ul class="pagination">
    <li{% if not pagination.has_prev %} class="disabled"{% endif %}>
        <a href="{% if pagination.has_prev %}{{ url_for(endpoint,
            page = pagination.page - 1, **kwargs) }}{% else %}#{% endif %}">
            &laquo;
        </a>
    </li>
    {% for p in pagination.iter_pages() %}
        {% if p %}
            {% if p == pagination.page %}
            <li class="active">
                <a href="{{ url_for(endpoint, page = p, **kwargs) }}">{{ p }}</a>
            </li>
            {% else %}
            <li>
                <a href="{{ url_for(endpoint, page = p, **kwargs) }}">{{ p }}</a>
            </li>
            {% endif %}
        {% else %}
        <li class="disabled"><a href="#">&hellip;</a></li>
        {% endif %}
    {% endfor %}
    <li{% if not pagination.has_next %} class="disabled"{% endif %}>
        <a href="{% if pagination.has_next %}{{ url_for(endpoint,
            page = pagination.page + 1, **kwargs) }}{% else %}#{% endif %}">
            &raquo;
        </a>
    </li>
```

```
</ul>
{% endmacro %}
```

The macro creates a Bootstrap pagination element, which is a styled unordered list. It defines the following page links inside it:

- A "previous page" link. This link gets the `disabled` class if the current page is the first page.

- Links to the all pages returned by the pagination object's `iter_pages()` iterator. These pages are rendered as links with an explicit page number, given as an argument to `url_for()`. The page currently displayed is highlighted using the `active` CSS class. Gaps in the sequence of pages are rendered with the ellipsis character.

- A "next page" link. This link will appear disabled if the current page is the last page.

Jinja2 macros always receive keyword arguments without having to include `**kwargs` in the argument list. The pagination macro passes all the keyword arguments it receives to the `url_for()` call that generates the pagination links. This approach can be used with routes such as the profile page that have a dynamic part.

The `pagination_widget` macro can be added below the *_posts.html* template included by *index.html* and *user.html*. Example 11-11 shows how it is used in the application's home page.

Example 11-11. app/templates/index.html: Pagination footer for blog post lists

```
{% extends "base.html" %}
{% import "bootstrap/wtf.html" as wtf %}
{% import "_macros.html" as macros %}
...
{% include '_posts.html' %}
<div class="pagination">
    {{ macros.pagination_widget(pagination, '.index') }}
</div>
{% endif %}
```

Figure 11-2 shows how the pagination links appear in the page.

 If you have cloned the application's Git repository on GitHub, you can run `git checkout 11d` to check out this version of the application.

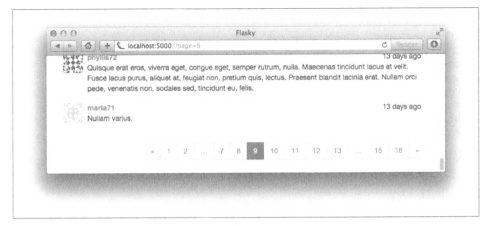

Figure 11-2. Blog post pagination

Rich-Text Posts with Markdown and Flask-PageDown

Plain-text posts are sufficient for short messages and status updates, but users who want to write longer articles will find the lack of formatting very limiting. In this section, the text area field where posts are entered will be upgraded to support the Markdown (*http://daringfireball.net/projects/markdown/*) syntax and present a rich-text preview of the post.

The implementation of this feature requires a few new packages:

- PageDown, a client-side Markdown-to-HTML converter implemented in Java-Script.
- Flask-PageDown, a PageDown wrapper for Flask that integrates PageDown with Flask-WTF forms.
- Markdown, a server-side Markdown-to-HTML converter implemented in Python.
- Bleach, an HTML sanitizer implemented in Python.

The Python packages can all be installed with pip:

```
(venv) $ pip install flask-pagedown markdown bleach
```

Using Flask-PageDown

The Flask-PageDown extension defines a `PageDownField` class that has the same inter-face as the `TextAreaField` from WTForms. Before this field can be used, the extension needs to be initialized as shown in Example 11-12.

Example 11-12. app/__init__.py: Flask-PageDown initialization

```
from flask.ext.pagedown import PageDown
# ...
pagedown = PageDown()
# ...
def create_app(config_name):
    # ...
    pagedown.init_app(app)
    # ...
```

To convert the text area control in the home page to a Markdown rich-text editor, the body field of the `PostForm` must be changed to a `PageDownField` as shown in Example 11-13.

Example 11-13. app/main/forms.py: Markdown-enabled post form

```
from flask.ext.pagedown.fields import PageDownField

class PostForm(Form):
    body = PageDownField("What's on your mind?", validators=[Required()])
    submit = SubmitField('Submit')
```

The Markdown preview is generated with the help of the PageDown libraries, so these must be added to the template. Flask-PageDown simplifies this task by providing a template macro that includes the required files from a CDN as shown in Example 11-14.

Example 11-14. app/index.html: Flask-PageDown template declaration

```
{% block scripts %}
{{ super() }}
{{ pagedown.include_pagedown() }}
{% endblock %}
```

 If you have cloned the application's Git repository on GitHub, you can run `git checkout 11e` to check out this version of the application. To ensure that you have all the dependencies installed also run `pip install -r requirements/dev.txt`.

With these changes, Markdown-formatted text typed in the text area field will be immediately rendered as HTML in the preview area below. Figure 11-3 shows the blog submission form with rich text.

Figure 11-3. Rich-text blog post form

Handling Rich Text on the Server

When the form is submitted only the raw Markdown text is sent with the POST request; the HTML preview that was shown on the page is discarded. Sending the generated HTML preview with the form can be considered a security risk, as it would be fairly easy for an attacker to construct HTML sequences that do not match the Markdown source and submit them. To avoid any risks, only the Markdown source text is submitted, and once in the server it is converted again to HTML using *Markdown*, a Python Markdown-to-HTML converter. The resulting HTML will be sanitized with *Bleach* to ensure that only a short list of allowed HTML tags are used.

The conversion of the Markdown blog posts to HTML can be issued in the *_posts.html* template, but this is inefficient, as posts will have to be converted every time they are rendered to a page. To avoid this repetition, the conversion can be done once when the blog post is created. The HTML code for the rendered blog post is *cached* in a new field added to the Post model that the template can access directly. The original Markdown source is also kept in the database in case the post needs to be edited. Example 11-15 shows the changes to the Post model.

Example 11-15. app/models/post.py: Markdown text handling in the Post model

```
from markdown import markdown
import bleach

class Post(db.Model):
    # ...
    body_html = db.Column(db.Text)
```

```
# ...
@staticmethod
def on_changed_body(target, value, oldvalue, initiator):
    allowed_tags = ['a', 'abbr', 'acronym', 'b', 'blockquote', 'code',
                    'em', 'i', 'li', 'ol', 'pre', 'strong', 'ul',
                    'h1', 'h2', 'h3', 'p']
    target.body_html = bleach.linkify(bleach.clean(
        markdown(value, output_format='html'),
        tags=allowed_tags, strip=True))

db.event.listen(Post.body, 'set', Post.on_changed_body)
```

The on_changed_body function is registered as a listener of SQLAlchemy's "set" event for body, which means that it will be automatically invoked whenever the body field on any instance of the class is set to a new value. The function renders the HTML version of the body and stores it in body_html, effectively making the conversion of the Markdown text to HTML fully automatic.

The actual conversion is done in three steps. First, the markdown() function does an initial conversion to HTML. The result is passed to clean(), along with the list of approved HTML tags. The clean() function removes any tags not on the white list. The final conversion is done with linkify(), another function provided by Bleach that converts any URLs written in plain text into proper <a> links. This last step is necessary because automatic link generation is not officially in the Markdown specification. PageDown supports it as an extension, so linkify() is used in the server to match.

The last change is to replace post.body with post.body_html in the template when available, as shown in Example 11-16.

Example 11-16. app/templates/_posts.html: Use the HTML version of the post bodies in the template

```
...
<div class="post-body">
    {% if post.body_html %}
        {{ post.body_html | safe }}
    {% else %}
        {{ post.body }}
    {% endif %}
</div>
...
```

The | safe suffix when rendering the HTML body is there to tell Jinja2 not to escape the HTML elements. Jinja2 escapes all template variables by default as a security measure. The Markdown-generated HTML was generated in the server, so it is safe to render.

If you have cloned the application's Git repository on GitHub, you can run `git checkout 11f` to check out this version of the application. This update also contains a database migration, so remember to run `python manage.py db upgrade` after you check out the code. To ensure that you have all the dependencies installed also run `pip install -r requirements/dev.txt`.

Permanent Links to Blog Posts

Users may want to share links to specific blog posts with friends on social networks. For this purpose, each post will be assigned a page with a unique URL that references it. The route and view function that support permanent links are shown in Example 11-17.

Example 11-17. app/main/views.py: Permanent links to posts

```
@main.route('/post/<int:id>')
def post(id):
    post = Post.query.get_or_404(id)
    return render_template('post.html', posts=[post])
```

The URLs that will be assigned to blog posts are constructed with the unique `id` field assigned when the post is inserted in the database.

For some types of applications, building permanent links that use readable URLs instead of numeric IDs may be preferred. An alternative to numeric IDs is to assign each blog post a *slug*, which is a unique string that is related to the post.

Note that the *post.html* template receives a list with just the post to render. Sending a list is necessary so that the *_posts.html* template referenced by *index.html* and *user.html* can be used in this page as well.

The permanent links are added at the bottom of each post in the generic *_posts.html* template, as shown in Example 11-18.

Example 11-18. app/templates/_posts.html: Permanent links to posts

```
<ul class="posts">
    {% for post in posts %}
    <li class="post">
        ...
        <div class="post-content">
            ...
            <div class="post-footer">
                <a href="{{ url_for('.post', id=post.id) }}">
                    <span class="label label-default">Permalink</span>
                </a>
```

```
            </div>
        </div>
    </li>
    {% endfor %}
</ul>
```

The new *post.html* template that renders the permanent link page is shown in Example 11-19. It includes the example template.

Example 11-19. app/templates/post.html: Permanent link template

```
{% extends "base.html" %}

{% block title %}Flasky - Post{% endblock %}

{% block page_content %}
{% include '_posts.html' %}
{% endblock %}
```

 If you have cloned the application's Git repository on GitHub, you can run `git checkout 11g` to check out this version of the application.

Blog Post Editor

The last feature related to blog posts is a post editor that allows users to edit their own posts. The blog post editor will live in a standalone page. At the top of the page, the current version of the post will be shown for reference, followed by a Markdown editor where the source Markdown can be modified. The editor will be based on Flask-PageDown, so a preview of the edited version of the blog post will be shown at the bottom of the page. The *edit_post.html* template is shown in Example 11-20.

Example 11-20. app/templates/edit_post.html: Edit blog post template

```
{% extends "base.html" %}
{% import "bootstrap/wtf.html" as wtf %}

{% block title %}Flasky - Edit Post{% endblock %}

{% block page_content %}
<div class="page-header">
    <h1>Edit Post</h1>
</div>
<div>
    {{ wtf.quick_form(form) }}
</div>
{% endblock %}
```

```
{% block scripts %}
{{ super() }}
{{ pagedown.include_pagedown() }}
{% endblock %}
```

The route that supports the blog post editor is shown in Example 11-21.

Example 11-21. app/main/views.py: Edit blog post route

```
@main.route('/edit/<int:id>', methods=['GET', 'POST'])
@login_required
def edit(id):
    post = Post.query.get_or_404(id)
    if current_user != post.author and \
            not current_user.can(Permission.ADMINISTER):
        abort(403)
    form = PostForm()
    if form.validate_on_submit():
        post.body = form.body.data
        db.session.add(post)
        flash('The post has been updated.')
        return redirect(url_for('post', id=post.id))
    form.body.data = post.body
    return render_template('edit_post.html', form=form)
```

This view function is coded to allow only the author of a blog post to edit it, except for administrators, who are allowed to edit posts from all users. If a user tries to edit a post from another user, the view function responds with a 403 code. The PostForm web form class used here is the same one used on the home page.

To complete the feature, a link to the blog post editor can be added below each blog post, next to the permanent link, as shown in Example 11-22.

Example 11-22. app/templates/_posts.html: Edit blog post links

```
<ul class="posts">
    {% for post in posts %}
    <li class="post">
        ...
        <div class="post-content">
            ...
            <div class="post-footer">
                ...
                {% if current_user == post.author %}
                <a href="{{ url_for('.edit', id=post.id) }}">
                    <span class="label label-primary">Edit</span>
                </a>
                {% elif current_user.is_administrator() %}
                <a href="{{ url_for('.edit', id=post.id) }}">
                    <span class="label label-danger">Edit [Admin]</span>
                </a>
                {% endif %}
```

```
        </div>
      </div>
    </li>
    {% endfor %}
</ul>
```

This change adds an "Edit" link to any blog posts that are authored by the current user. For administrators, the link is added to all posts. The administrator link is styled differently as a visual cue that this is an administration feature. Figure 11-4 shows how the Edit and Permalink links look in the web browser.

If you have cloned the application's Git repository on GitHub, you can run `git checkout 11h` to check out this version of the application.

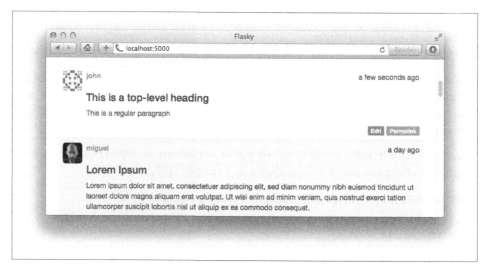

Figure 11-4. Edit and Permalink links in blog posts.

## CHAPTER 12

Followers

Socially aware web applications allow users to connect with other users. Applications call these relationships *followers*, *friends*, *contacts*, *connections*, or *buddies*, but the feature is the same regardless of the name, and in all cases involves keeping track of directional links between pairs of users and using these links in database queries.

In this chapter, you will learn how to implement a follower feature for Flasky. Users will be able to "follow" other users and choose to filter the blog post list on the home page to include only those from the users they follow.

Database Relationships Revisited

As we discussed in Chapter 5, databases establish links between records using *relationships*. The one-to-many relationship is the most common type of relationship, where a record is linked with a list of related records. To implement this type of relationship, the elements in the "many" side have a foreign key that points to the linked element on the "one" side. The example application in its current state includes two one-to-many relationships: one that links user roles to lists of users and another that links users to the blog posts they authored.

Most other relationship types can be derived from the one-to-many type. The *many-to-one* relationship is a one-to-many looked at from the point of view of the "many" side. The *one-to-one* relationship type is a simplification of the one-to-many, where the "many" side is constrained to only have at most one element. The only relationship type that cannot be implemented as a simple variation of the one-to-many model is the *many-to-many*, which has lists of elements on both sides. This relationship is described in detail in the following section.

Many-to-Many Relationships

The one-to-many, many-to-one, and one-to-one relationships all have at least one side with a single entity, so the links between related records are implemented with foreign keys pointing to that one element. But how do you implement a relationship where both sides are "many" sides?

Consider the classical example of a many-to-many relationship: a database of students and the classes they are taking. Clearly, you can't add a foreign key to a class in the students table, because a student takes many classes—one foreign key is not enough. Likewise, you cannot add a foreign key to the student in the classes table, because classes have more than one student. Both sides need a list of foreign keys.

The solution is to add a third table to the database, called an *association table*. Now the many-to-many relationship can be decomposed into two one-to-many relationships from each of the two original tables to the association table. Figure 12-1 shows how the many-to-many relationship between students and classes is represented.

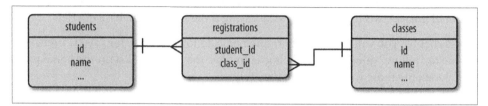

Figure 12-1. Many-to-many relationship example

The association table in this example is called `registrations`. Each row in this table represents an individual registration of a student in a class.

Querying a many-to-many relationship is a two-step process. To obtain the list of classes a student is taking, you start from the one-to-many relationship between students and registrations and get the list of registrations for the desired student. Then the one-to-many relationship between classes and registrations is traversed in the many-to-one direction to obtain all the classes associated with the registrations retrieved for the student. Likewise, to find all the students in a class, you start from the class and get a list of registrations, then get the students linked to those registrations.

Traversing two relationships to obtain query results sounds difficult, but for a simple relationship like the one in the previous example, SQLAlchemy does most of the work. Following is the code that represents the many-to-many relationship in Figure 12-1:

```
registrations = db.Table('registrations',
    db.Column('student_id', db.Integer, db.ForeignKey('students.id')),
    db.Column('class_id', db.Integer, db.ForeignKey('classes.id'))
)
```

```
class Student(db.Model):
    id = db.Column(db.Integer, primary_key=True)
    name = db.Column(db.String)
    classes = db.relationship('Class',
                              secondary=registrations,
                              backref=db.backref('students', lazy='dynamic'),
                              lazy='dynamic')

class Class(db.Model):
    id = db.Column(db.Integer, primary_key = True)
    name = db.Column(db.String)
```

The relationship is defined with the same db.relationship() construct that is used for one-to-many relationships, but in the case of a many-to-many relationship the additional secondary argument must to be set to the association table. The relationship can be defined in either one of the two classes, with the backref argument taking care of exposing the relationship from the other side as well. The association table is defined as a simple table, not as a model, since SQLAlchemy manages this table internally.

The classes relationship uses list semantics, which makes working with a many-to-many relationships configured in this way extremely easy. Given a student s and a class c, the code that registers the student for the class is:

```
>>> s.classes.append(c)
>>> db.session.add(s)
```

The queries that list the classes student s is registered for and the list of students registered for class c are also very simple:

```
>>> s.classes.all()
>>> c.students.all()
```

The students relationship available in the Class model is the one defined in the db.backref() argument. Note that in this relationship the backref argument was expanded to also have a lazy = 'dynamic' attribute, so both sides return a query that can accept additional filters.

If student s later decides to drop class c, you can update the database as follows:

```
>>> s.classes.remove(c)
```

Self-Referential Relationships

A many-to-many relationship can be used to model users following other users, but there is a problem. In the example of students and classes, there were two very clearly defined entities linked together by the association table. However, to represent users following other users, it is just users—there is no second entity.

A relationship in which both sides belong to the same table is said to be *self-referential*. In this case the entities on the left side of the relationship are users, which can be called the "followers." The entities on the right side are also users, but these are the "followed" users. Conceptually, self-referential relationships are no different than regular relationships, but they are harder to think about. Figure 12-2 shows a database diagram for a self-referential relationship that represents users following other users.

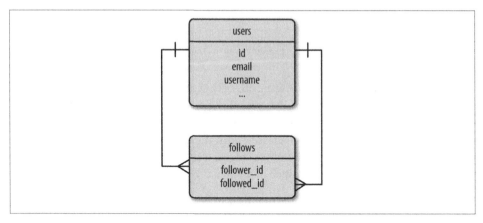

Figure 12-2. Followers, many-to-many relationship

The association table in this case is called follows. Each row in this table represents a user following another user. The one-to-many relationship pictured on the left side associates users with the list of "follows" rows in which they are the followers. The one-to-many relationship pictured on the right side associates users with the list of "follows" rows in which they are the followed user.

Advanced Many-to-Many Relationships

With a self-referential many-to-many relationship configured as indicated in the previous example, the database can represent followers, but there is one limitation. A common need when working with many-to-many relationships is to store additional data that applies to the link between two entities. For the followers relationship, it can be useful to store the date a user started following another user, as that will enable lists of followers to be presented in chronological order. The only place this information can be stored is in the association table, but in an implementation similar to that of the students and classes shown earlier, the association table is an internal table that is fully managed by SQLAlchemy.

To be able to work with custom data in the relationship, the association table must be promoted to a proper model that the application can access. Example 12-1 shows the new association table, represented by the Follow model.

Example 12-1. app/models/user.py: The follows association table as a model

```
class Follow(db.Model):
    __tablename__ = 'follows'
    follower_id = db.Column(db.Integer, db.ForeignKey('users.id'),
                            primary_key=True)
    followed_id = db.Column(db.Integer, db.ForeignKey('users.id'),
                            primary_key=True)
    timestamp = db.Column(db.DateTime, default=datetime.utcnow)
```

SQLAlchemy cannot use the association table transparently because that will not give the application access to the custom fields in it. Instead, the many-to-many relationship must be decomposed into the two basic one-to-many relationships for the left and right sides, and these must be defined as standard relationships. This is shown in Example 12-2.

Example 12-2. app/models/user.py: A many-to-many relationship implemented as two one-to-many relationships

```
class User(UserMixin, db.Model):
    # ...
    followed = db.relationship('Follow',
                               foreign_keys=[Follow.follower_id],
                               backref=db.backref('follower', lazy='joined'),
                               lazy='dynamic',
                               cascade='all, delete-orphan')
    followers = db.relationship('Follow',
                                foreign_keys=[Follow.followed_id],
                                backref=db.backref('followed', lazy='joined'),
                                lazy='dynamic',
                                cascade='all, delete-orphan')
```

Here the `followed` and `followers` relationships are defined as individual one-to-many relationships. Note that it is necessary to eliminate any ambiguity between foreign keys by specifying in each relationship which foreign key to use through the `foreign_keys` optional argument. The `db.backref()` arguments in these relationships do not apply to each other; the back references are applied to the `Follow` model.

The `lazy` argument for the back references is specified as `joined`. This lazy mode causes the related object to be loaded immediately from the join query. For example, if a user is following 100 other users, calling `user.followed.all()` will return a list of 100 `Follow` instances, where each one has the `follower` and `followed` back reference properties set to the respective users. The `lazy='joined'` mode enables this all to happen from a single database query. If `lazy` is set to the default value of `select`, then the `follower` and `followed` users are loaded lazily when they are first accessed and each attribute will require an individual query, which means that obtaining the complete list of followed users would require 100 additional database queries.

The `lazy` argument on the `User` side of both relationships has different needs. These are on the "one" side and return the "many" side; here a mode of `dynamic` is used, so that the relationship attributes return query objects instead of returning the items directly, so that additional filters can be added to the query before it is executed.

The `cascade` argument configures how actions performed on a parent object propagate to related objects. An example of a cascade option is the rule that says that when an object is added to the database session, any objects associated with it through relationships should automatically be added to the session as well. The default cascade options are appropriate for most situations, but there is one case in which the default cascade options do not work well for this many-to-many relationship. The default cascade behavior when an object is deleted is to set the foreign key in any related objects that link to it to a null value. But for an association table, the correct behavior is to delete the entries that point to a record that was deleted, as this effectively destroys the link. This is what the `delete-orphan` cascade option does.

 The value given to `cascade` is a comma-separated list of cascade options. This is somewhat confusing, but the option named `all` represents all the cascade options except `delete-orphan`. Using the value `all, delete-orphan` leaves the default cascade options enabled and adds the delete behavior for orphans.

The application now needs to work with the two one-to-many relationships to implement the many-to-many functionality. Since these are operations that will need to be repeated often, it is a good idea to create helper methods in the `User` model for all the possible operations. The four new methods that control this relationship are shown in Example 12-3.

Example 12-3. app/models/user.py: Followers helper methods

```
class User(db.Model):
    # ...
    def follow(self, user):
        if not self.is_following(user):
            f = Follow(follower=self, followed=user)
            db.session.add(f)

    def unfollow(self, user):
        f = self.followed.filter_by(followed_id=user.id).first()
        if f:
            db.session.delete(f)

    def is_following(self, user):
        return self.followed.filter_by(
            followed_id=user.id).first() is not None

    def is_followed_by(self, user):
```

```
    return self.followers.filter_by(
        follower_id=user.id).first() is not None
```

The `follow()` method manually inserts a `Follow` instance in the association table that links a follower with a followed user, giving the application the opportunity to set the custom field. The two users who are connecting are manually assigned to the new `Follow` instance in its constructor, and then the object is added to the database session as usual. Note that there is no need to manually set the `timestamp` field because it was defined with a default value that sets the current date and time. The `unfollow()` method uses the `followed` relationship to locate the `Follow` instance that links the user to the followed user who needs to be disconnected. To destroy the link between the two users, the `Follow` object is simply deleted. The `is_following()` and `is_followed_by()` methods search the left-and right-side one-to-many relationships respectively for the given user and return `True` if the user is found.

 If you have cloned the application's Git repository on GitHub, you can run `git checkout 12a` to check out this version of the application. This update contains a database migration, so remember to run `python manage.py db upgrade` after you check out the code.

The database part of the feature is now complete. You can find a unit test that exercises the database relationship in the source code repository on GitHub.

Followers on the Profile Page

The profile page of a user needs to present a "Follow" button if the user viewing it is not a follower, or an "Unfollow" button if the user is a follower. It is also a nice addition to show the follower and followed counts, display the lists of followers and followed users, and show a "Follows You" sign when appropriate. The changes to the user profile template are shown in Example 12-4. Figure 12-3 shows how the additions look on the profile page.

Example 12-4. app/templates/user.html: Follower enhancements to the user profile header

```
{% if current_user.can(Permission.FOLLOW) and user != current_user %}
    {% if not current_user.is_following(user) %}
    <a href="{{ url_for('.follow', username=user.username) }}"
        class="btn btn-primary">Follow</a>
    {% else %}
    <a href="{{ url_for('.unfollow', username=user.username) }}"
        class="btn btn-default">Unfollow</a>
    {% endif %}
{% endif %}
<a href="{{ url_for('.followers', username=user.username) }}">
```

```
    Followers: <span class="badge">{{ user.followers.count() }}</span>
</a>
<a href="{{ url_for('.followed_by', username=user.username) }}">
    Following: <span class="badge">{{ user.followed.count() }}</span>
</a>
{% if current_user.is_authenticated() and user != current_user and
    user.is_following(current_user) %}
| <span class="label label-default">Follows you</span>
{% endif %}
```

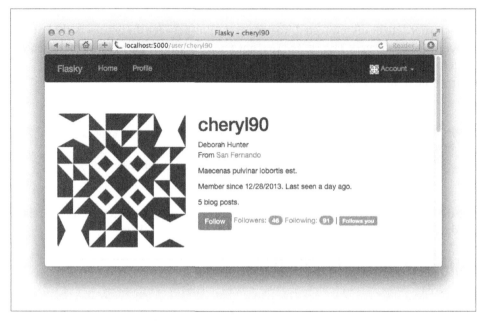

Figure 12-3. Followers on the profile page

There are four new endpoints defined in these template changes. The */follow/<user-name>* route is invoked when a user clicks the "Follow" button on another user's profile page. The implementation is shown in Example 12-5.

Example 12-5. app/main/views.py: Follow route and view function

```python
@main.route('/follow/<username>')
@login_required
@permission_required(Permission.FOLLOW)
def follow(username):
    user = User.query.filter_by(username=username).first()
    if user is None:
        flash('Invalid user.')
        return redirect(url_for('.index'))
    if current_user.is_following(user):
        flash('You are already following this user.')
```

```
        return redirect(url_for('.user', username=username))
    current_user.follow(user)
    flash('You are now following %s.' % username)
    return redirect(url_for('.user', username=username))
```

This view function loads the requested user, verifies that it is valid and that it isn't already followed by the logged-in user, and then calls the follow() helper function in the User model to establish the link. The /unfollow/<username> route is implemented in a similar way.

The /followers/<username> route is invoked when a user clicks another user's follower count on the profile page. The implementation is shown in Example 12-6.

Example 12-6. app/main/views.py: Followers route and view function

```
@main.route('/followers/<username>')
def followers(username):
    user = User.query.filter_by(username=username).first()
    if user is None:
        flash('Invalid user.')
        return redirect(url_for('.index'))
    page = request.args.get('page', 1, type=int)
    pagination = user.followers.paginate(
        page, per_page=current_app.config['FLASKY_FOLLOWERS_PER_PAGE'],
        error_out=False)
    follows = [{'user': item.follower, 'timestamp': item.timestamp}
                for item in pagination.items]
    return render_template('followers.html', user=user, title="Followers of",
                            endpoint='.followers', pagination=pagination,
                            follows=follows)
```

This function loads and validates the requested user, then paginates its followers relationship using the same techniques learned in Chapter 11. Because the query for followers returns Follow instances, the list is converted into another list that has user and timestamp fields in each entry so that rendering is simpler.

The template that renders the follower list can be written generically so that it can be used for lists of followers and followed users. The template receives the user, a title for the page, the endpoint to use in the pagination links, the pagination object, and the list of results.

The followed_by endpoint is almost identical. The only difference is that the list of users is obtained from the user.followed relationship. The template arguments are also adjusted accordingly.

The *followers.html* template is implemented with a two-column table that shows usernames and their avatars on the left and Flask-Moment timestamps on the right. You can consult the source code repository on GitHub to study the implementation in detail.

If you have cloned the application's Git repository on GitHub, you can run `git checkout 12b` to check out this version of the application.

Query Followed Posts Using a Database Join

The application's home page currently shows all the posts in the database in descending chronological order. With the followers feature now complete, it would be a nice addition to give users the option to view blog posts from only the users they follow.

The obvious way to load all the posts authored by followed users is to first get the list of those users and then get the posts from each and sort them into a single list. Of course that approach does not scale well; the effort to obtain this combined list will grow as the database grows, and operations such as pagination cannot be done efficiently. The key to obtaining the blog posts with good performance is doing it with a single query.

The database operation that can do this is called a *join*. A join operation takes two or more tables and finds all the combination of rows that satisfy a given condition. The resulted combined rows are inserted into a temporary table that is the result of the join. The best way to explain how joins work is through an example.

Table 12-1 shows an example `users` table with three users.

Table 12-1. users table

id	username
1	john
2	susan
3	david

Table 12-2 shows the corresponding `posts` table, with some blog posts.

Table 12-2. Posts table

id	author_id	body
1	2	Blog post by susan
2	1	Blog post by john
3	3	Blog post by david
4	1	Second blog post by john

Finally, Table 12-3 shows who is following whom. In this table you can see that *john* is following *david*, *susan* is following *john*, and *david* is not following anyone.

Table 12-3. Follows table

follower_id	followed_id
1	3
2	1
2	3

To obtain the list of posts followed by user *susan*, the `posts` and `follows` tables must be combined. First the `follows` table is filtered to keep just the rows that have *susan* as the follower, which in this example are the last two rows. Then a temporary join table is created from all the possible combinations of rows from the `posts` and filtered `follows` tables in which the `author_id` of the post is the same as the `followed_id` of the follow, effectively selecting any posts that appear in the list of users *susan* is following. Table 12-4 shows the result of the join operation. The columns that were used to perform the join are marked with * in this table.

Table 12-4. Joined table

id	author_id*	body	follower_id	followed_id*
2	1	Blog post by john	2	1
3	3	Blog post by david	2	3
4	1	Second blog post by john	2	1

This table contains exactly the list of blog posts authored by users that *susan* is following. The Flask-SQLAlchemy query that literally performs the join operation as described is fairly complex:

```
return db.session.query(Post).select_from(Follow).\
    filter_by(follower_id=self.id).\
    join(Post, Follow.followed_id == Post.author_id)
```

All the queries that you have seen so far start from the `query` attribute of the model that is queried. That format does not work well for this query, because the query needs to return `posts` rows, yet the first operation that needs to be done is to apply a filter to the `follows` table. So a more basic form of the query is used instead. To fully understand this query, each part should be looked at individually:

- `db.session.query(Post)` specifies that this is going to be a query that returns `Post` objects.
- `select_from(Follow)` says that the query begins with the `Follow` model.
- `filter_by(follower_id=self.id)` performs the filtering of the `follows` table by the follower user.

- join(Post, Follow.followed_id == Post.author_id) joins the results of filter_by() with the Post objects.

The query can be simplified by swapping the order of the filter and the join:

```
return Post.query.join(Follow, Follow.followed_id == Post.author_id)\
    .filter(Follow.follower_id == self.id)
```

By issuing the join operation first, the query can be started from Post.query, so now the only two filters that need to be applied are join() and filter(). But is this the same? It may seem that doing the join first and then the filtering would be more work, but in reality these two queries are equivalent. SQLAlchemy first collects all the filters and then generates the query in the most efficient way. The native SQL instructions for these two queries are identical. The final version of this query is added to the Post model, as shown in Example 12-7.

Example 12-7. app/models/user.py: Obtain followed posts

```
class User(db.Model):
    # ...
    @property
    def followed_posts(self):
        return Post.query.join(Follow, Follow.followed_id == Post.author_id)\
            .filter(Follow.follower_id == self.id)
```

Note that the followed_posts() method is defined as a property so that it does not need the (). That way, all relationships have a consistent syntax.

 If you have cloned the application's Git repository on GitHub, you can run git checkout 12c to check out this version of the application.

Joins are extremely hard to wrap your head around; you may need to experiment with the example code in a shell before it all sinks in.

Show Followed Posts on the Home Page

The home page can now give users the choice to view all blog posts or just those from followed users. Example 12-8 shows how this choice is implemented.

Example 12-8. app/main/views.py: Show all or followed posts

```
@app.route('/', methods = ['GET', 'POST'])
def index():
    # ...
    show_followed = False
```

```
if current_user.is_authenticated():
    show_followed = bool(request.cookies.get('show_followed', ''))
if show_followed:
    query = current_user.followed_posts
else:
    query = Post.query
pagination = query.order_by(Post.timestamp.desc()).paginate(
    page, per_page=current_app.config['FLASKY_POSTS_PER_PAGE'],
    error_out=False)
posts = pagination.items
return render_template('index.html', form=form, posts=posts,
                       show_followed=show_followed, pagination=pagination)
```

The choice of showing all or followed posts is stored in a cookie called show_followed that when set to a nonempty string indicates that only followed posts should be shown. Cookies are stored in the request object as a request.cookies dictionary. The string value of the cookie is converted to a Boolean, and based on its value a query local variable is set to the query that obtains the complete or filtered lists of blog posts. To show all the posts, the top-level query Post.query is used, and the recently added User.followed_posts property is used when the list should be restricted to followers. The query stored in the query local variable is then paginated and the results sent to the template as before.

The show_followed cookie is set in two new routes, shown in Example 12-9.

Example 12-9. app/main/views.py: Selection of all or followed posts

```
@main.route('/all')
@login_required
def show_all():
    resp = make_response(redirect(url_for('.index')))
    resp.set_cookie('show_followed', '', max_age=30*24*60*60)
    return resp

@main.route('/followed')
@login_required
def show_followed():
    resp = make_response(redirect(url_for('.index')))
    resp.set_cookie('show_followed', '1', max_age=30*24*60*60)
    return resp
```

Links to these routes are added to the home page template. When they are invoked, the show_followed cookie is set to the proper value and a redirect back to the home page is issued.

Cookies can be set only on a response object, so these routes need to create a response object through make_response() instead of letting Flask do this.

The set_cookie() function takes the cookie name and the value as the first two arguments. The max_age optional argument sets the number of seconds until the cookie expires. Not including this argument makes the cookie expire when the browser window is closed. In this case, an age of 30 days is set so that the setting is remembered even if the user does not return to the application for several days.

The changes to the template add two navigation tabs at the top of the page that invoke the */all* or */followed* routes to set the correct settings in the session. You can inspect the template changes in detail in the source code repository on GitHub. Figure 12-4 shows how the home page looks with these changes.

Figure 12-4. Followed posts on the home page

 If you have cloned the application's Git repository on GitHub, you can run `git checkout 12d` to check out this version of the application.

If you try the application at this point and switch to the followed list of posts, you will notice that your own posts do not appear in the list. This is of course correct, because users are not followers of themselves.

Even though the queries are working as designed, most users will expect to see their own posts when they are looking at those of their friends. The easiest way to address this issue is to register all users as their own followers at the time they are created. This trick is shown in Example 12-10.

Example 12-10. app/models/user.py: Make users their own followers on construction

```
class User(UserMixin, db.Model):
    # ...
    def __init__(self, **kwargs):
        # ...
        self.follow(self)
```

Unfortunately, you likely have several users in the database who are already created and are not following themselves. If the database is small and easy to regenerate, then it can be deleted and re-created, but if that is not an option, then adding an update function that fixes existing users is the proper solution. This is shown in Example 12-11.

Example 12-11. app/models/user.py: Make users their own followers

```
class User(UserMixin, db.Model):
    # ...
    @staticmethod
    def add_self_follows():
        for user in User.query.all():
            if not user.is_following(user):
                user.follow(user)
                db.session.add(user)
                db.session.commit()
    # ...
```

Now the database can be updated by running the previous example function from the shell:

```
(venv) $ python manage.py shell
>>> User.add_self_follows()
```

Creating functions that introduce updates to the database is a common technique used to update applications that are deployed, as running a scripted update is less error prone than updating databases manually. In Chapter 17 you will see how this function and others like it can be incorporated into a deployment script.

Making all users self-followers makes the application more usable, but this change introduces a few complications. The follower and followed user counts shown in the user profile page are now increased by one due to the self-follower links. The numbers need to be decreased by one to be accurate, which is easy to do directly in the template by rendering {{ user.followers.count() - 1 }} and {{ user.followed.count() - 1 }}. The lists of follower and followed users also must be adjusted to not show the same user, another simple task to do in the template with a conditional. Finally, any unit tests that check follower counts are also affected by the self-follower links and must be adjusted to account for the self-followers.

If you have cloned the application's Git repository on GitHub, you can run `git checkout 12e` to check out this version of the application.

In the next chapter, the user comment subsystem will be implemented—another very important feature of socially aware applications.

## CHAPTER 13

User Comments

Allowing users to interact is key to the success of a social blogging platform. In this chapter, you will learn how to implement user comments. The techniques presented are generic enough to be directly applicable to a large number of socially enabled applications.

Database Representation of Comments

Comments are not very different from blog posts. Both have a body, an author, and a timestamp, and in this particular implementation both are written with Markdown syntax. Figure 13-1 shows a diagram of the comments table and its relationships with other tables in the database.

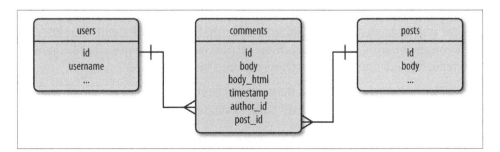

Figure 13-1. Database representation of blog post comments

Comments apply specific blog posts, so a one-to-many relationship from the posts table is defined. This relationship can be used to obtain the list of comments associated with a particular blog post.

The `comments` table is also in a one-to-many relationship with the `users` table. This relationship gives access to all the comments made by a user, and indirectly how many comments a user has written, a piece of information that can be interesting to show in user profile pages. The definition of the `Comment` model is shown in Example 13-1.

Example 13-1. app/models.py: Comment model

```
class Comment(db.Model):
    __tablename__ = 'comments'
    id = db.Column(db.Integer, primary_key=True)
    body = db.Column(db.Text)
    body_html = db.Column(db.Text)
    timestamp = db.Column(db.DateTime, index=True, default=datetime.utcnow)
    disabled = db.Column(db.Boolean)
    author_id = db.Column(db.Integer, db.ForeignKey('users.id'))
    post_id = db.Column(db.Integer, db.ForeignKey('posts.id'))

    @staticmethod
    def on_changed_body(target, value, oldvalue, initiator):
        allowed_tags = ['a', 'abbr', 'acronym', 'b', 'code', 'em', 'i',
                        'strong']
        target.body_html = bleach.linkify(bleach.clean(
            markdown(value, output_format='html'),
            tags=allowed_tags, strip=True))

db.event.listen(Comment.body, 'set', Comment.on_changed_body)
```

The attributes of the `Comment` model are almost the same as those of `Post`. One addition is the `disabled` field, a Boolean that will be used by moderators to suppress comments that are inappropriate or offensive. As was done for blog posts, comments define an event that triggers any time the body field changes, automating the rendering of the Markdown text to HTML. The process is identical to what was done for blog posts in Chapter 11, but since comments tend to be short, the list of HTML tags that are allowed in the conversion from Markdown is more restrictive, the paragraph-related tags have been removed, and only the character formatting tags are left.

To complete the database changes, the `User` and `Post` models must define the one-to-many relationships with the `comments` table, as shown in Example 13-2.

Example 13-2. app/models/user.py: One-to-many relationships from users and posts to comments

```
class User(db.Model):
    # ...
    comments = db.relationship('Comment', backref='author', lazy='dynamic')

class Post(db.Model):
    # ...
    comments = db.relationship('Comment', backref='post', lazy='dynamic')
```

Comment Submission and Display

In this application, comments are displayed in the individual blog post pages that were added as permanent links in Chapter 11. A submission form is also included on this page. Example 13-3 shows the web form that will be used to enter comments—an extremely simple form that only has a text field and a submit button.

Example 13-3. app/main/forms.py: Comment input form

```
class CommentForm(Form):
    body = StringField('', validators=[Required()])
    submit = SubmitField('Submit')
```

Example 13-4 shows the updated */post/<int:id>* route with support for comments.

Example 13-4. app/main/views.py: Blog post comments support

```
@main.route('/post/<int:id>', methods=['GET', 'POST'])
def post(id):
    post = Post.query.get_or_404(id)
    form = CommentForm()
    if form.validate_on_submit():
        comment = Comment(body=form.body.data,
                          post=post,
                          author=current_user._get_current_object())
        db.session.add(comment)
        flash('Your comment has been published.')
        return redirect(url_for('.post', id=post.id, page=-1))
    page = request.args.get('page', 1, type=int)
    if page == -1:
        page = (post.comments.count() - 1) / \
                current_app.config['FLASKY_COMMENTS_PER_PAGE'] + 1
    pagination = post.comments.order_by(Comment.timestamp.asc()).paginate(
        page, per_page=current_app.config['FLASKY_COMMENTS_PER_PAGE'],
        error_out=False)
    comments = pagination.items
    return render_template('post.html', posts=[post], form=form,
                           comments=comments, pagination=pagination)
```

This view function instantiates the comment form and sends it to the *post.html* template for rendering. The logic that inserts a new comment when the form is submitted is similar to the handling of blog posts. As in the Post case, the author of the comment cannot be set directly to current_user because this is a context variable proxy object. The expression current_user._get_current_object() returns the actual User object.

The comments are sorted by their timestamp in chronological order, so new comments are always added at the bottom of the list. When a new comment is entered, the redirect that ends the request goes back to the same URL, but the url_for() function sets the page to -1, a special page number that is used to request the last page of comments so that the comment just entered is seen on the page. When the page number is obtained from the query string and found to be -1, a calculation with the number of comments and the page size is done to obtain the actual page number to use.

The list of comments associated with the post are obtained through the post.comments one-to-many relationship, sorted by comment timestamp, and paginated with the same techniques used for blog posts. The comments and the pagination object are sent to the template for rendering. The FLASKY_COMMENTS_PER_PAGE configuration variable is added to *config.py* to control the size of each page of comments.

The comment rendering is defined in a new template *_comments.html* that is similar to *_posts.html* but uses a different set of CSS classes. This template is included by *_post.html* below the body of the post, followed by a call to the pagination macro. You can review the changes to the templates in the application's GitHub repository.

To complete this feature, blog posts shown in the home and profile pages need a link to the page with the comments. This is shown in Example 13-5.

Example 13-5. _app/templates/_posts.html: Link to blog post comments

```
<a href="{{ url_for('.post', id=post.id) }}#comments">
    <span class="label label-primary">
        {{ post.comments.count() }} Comments
    </span>
</a>
```

Note how the text of the link includes the number of comments, which is easily obtained from the one-to-many relationship between the posts and comments tables using SQLAlchemy's count() filter.

Also of interest is the structure of the link to the comments page, which is built as the permanent link for the post with a *#comments* suffix added. This last part is called a *URL fragment* and is used to indicate an initial scroll position for the page. The web browser looks for an element with the id given and scrolls the page so that the element appears at the top of the page. This initial position is set to the comments heading in the *post.html* template, which is written as <h4 id="comments">Comments<h4>. Figure 13-2 shows how the comments appear on the page.

An additional change was made to the pagination macro. The pagination links for comments also need the *#comments* fragment added, so a fragment argument was added to the macro and passed in the macro invocation from the *post.html* template.

If you have cloned the application's Git repository on GitHub, you can run git checkout 13a to check out this version of the application. This update contains a database migration, so remember to run python manage.py db upgrade after you check out the code.

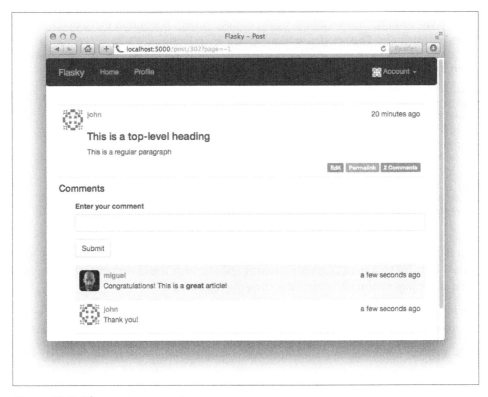

Figure 13-2. Blog post comments

Comment Moderation

In Chapter 9 a list of user roles was defined, each with a list of permissions. One of the permissions was `Permission.MODERATE_COMMENTS`, which gives users who have it in their roles the power to moderate comments made by others.

This feature will be exposed as a link in the navigation bar that appears only to users who are permitted to use it. This is done in the *base.html* template using a conditional, as shown in Example 13-6.

Example 13-6. app/templates/base.html: Moderate comments link in navigation bar

```
...
{% if current_user.can(Permission.MODERATE_COMMENTS) %}
<li><a href="{{ url_for('main.moderate') }}">Moderate Comments</a></li>
{% endif %}
...
```

The moderation page shows the comments for all the posts in the same list, with the most recent comments shown first. Below each comment is a button that can toggle the disabled attribute. The /moderate route is shown in Example 13-7.

Example 13-7. app/main/views.py: Comment moderation route

```
@main.route('/moderate')
@login_required
@permission_required(Permission.MODERATE_COMMENTS)
def moderate():
    page = request.args.get('page', 1, type=int)
    pagination = Comment.query.order_by(Comment.timestamp.desc()).paginate(
        page, per_page=current_app.config['FLASKY_COMMENTS_PER_PAGE'],
        error_out=False)
    comments = pagination.items
    return render_template('moderate.html', comments=comments,
                           pagination=pagination, page=page)
```

This is a very simple function that reads a page of comments from the database and passes them on to a template for rendering. Along with the comments, the template receives the pagination object and the current page number.

The *moderate.html* template, shown in Example 13-8, is also simple because it relies on the *_comments.html* subtemplate created earlier for the rendering of the comments.

Example 13-8. app/templates/moderate.html: Comment moderation template

```
{% extends "base.html" %}
{% import "_macros.html" as macros %}

{% block title %}Flasky - Comment Moderation{% endblock %}

{% block page_content %}
<div class="page-header">
    <h1>Comment Moderation</h1>
</div>
{% set moderate = True %}
{% include '_comments.html' %}
{% if pagination %}
<div class="pagination">
    {{ macros.pagination_widget(pagination, '.moderate') }}
</div>
{% endif %}
{% endblock %}
```

This template defers the rendering of the comments to the *_comments.html* template, but before it hands control to the subordinate template it uses Jinja2's set directive to define a moderate template variable set to True. This variable is used by the *_comments.html* template to determine whether the moderation features need to be rendered.

The portion of the _comments.html_ template that renders the body of each comment needs to be modified in two ways. For regular users (when the `moderate` variable is not set), any comments that are marked as disabled should be suppressed. For moderators (when `moderate` is set to `True`), the body of the comment must be rendered regardless of the disabled state, and below the body a button should be included to toggle the state. Example 13-9 shows these changes.

_Example 13-9. app/templates/_comments.html: Rendering of the comment bodies_

```
...
<div class="comment-body">
    {% if comment.disabled %}
    <p></p><i>This comment has been disabled by a moderator.</i></p>
    {% endif %}
    {% if moderate or not comment.disabled %}
        {% if comment.body_html %}
            {{ comment.body_html | safe }}
        {% else %}
            {{ comment.body }}
        {% endif %}
    {% endif %}
</div>
{% if moderate %}
    <br>
    {% if comment.disabled %}
    <a class="btn btn-default btn-xs" href="{{ url_for('.moderate_enable',
        id=comment.id, page=page) }}">Enable</a>
    {% else %}
    <a class="btn btn-danger btn-xs" href="{{ url_for('.moderate_disable',
        id=comment.id, page=page) }}">Disable</a>
    {% endif %}
{% endif %}
...
```

With these changes, users will see a short notice for disabled comments. Moderators will see both the notice and the comment body. Moderators will also see a button to toggle the disabled state below each comment. The button invokes one of two new routes, depending on which of the two possible states the comment is changing to. Example 13-10 shows how these routes are defined.

Example 13-10. app/main/views.py: Comment moderation routes

```
@main.route('/moderate/enable/<int:id>')
@login_required
@permission_required(Permission.MODERATE_COMMENTS)
def moderate_enable(id):
    comment = Comment.query.get_or_404(id)
    comment.disabled = False
    db.session.add(comment)
    return redirect(url_for('.moderate',
                            page=request.args.get('page', 1, type=int)))
```

```
@main.route('/moderate/disable/<int:id>')
@login_required
@permission_required(Permission.MODERATE_COMMENTS)
def moderate_disable(id):
    comment = Comment.query.get_or_404(id)
    comment.disabled = True
    db.session.add(comment)
    return redirect(url_for('.moderate',
                            page=request.args.get('page', 1, type=int)))
```

The comment enable and disable routes load the comment object, set the `disabled` field
to the proper value, and write it back to the database. At the end, they redirect back to
the comment moderation page (shown in Figure 13-3), and if a `page` argument was
given in the query string, they include it in the redirect. The buttons in the _comments.html_ template were rendered with the page argument so that the redirect brings
the user back to the same page.

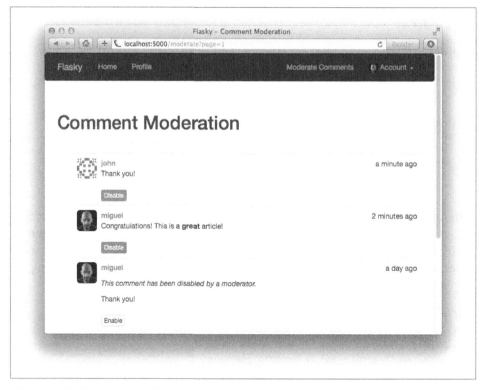

Figure 13-3. Comment moderation page

If you have cloned the application's Git repository on GitHub, you can run `git checkout 13b` to check out this version of the application.

The topic of social features is completed with this chapter. In the next chapter, you will learn how to expose the application functionality as an API that clients other than web browsers can use.

## CHAPTER 14

Application Programming Interfaces

In recent years, there has been a trend in web applications to move more and more of the business logic to the client side, producing an architecture that is known as Rich Internet Application (RIA). In RIAs, the server's main (and sometimes only) function is to provide the client application with data retrieval and storage services. In this model, the server becomes a *web service* or *Application Programming Interface (API)*.

There are several protocols by which RIAs can communicate with a web service. Remote Procedure Call (RPC) protocols such as XML-RPC or its derivative Simplified Object Access Protocol (SOAP) were popular choices a few years ago. More recently, the Representational State Transfer (REST) architecture has emerged as the favorite for web applications due to it being built on the familiar model of the World Wide Web.

Flask is an ideal framework to build *RESTful* web services due to its lightweight nature. In this chapter, you will learn how to implement a Flask-based RESTful API.

Introduction to REST

Roy Fielding's Ph.D. dissertation (*http://bit.ly/REST-fielding*) introduces the REST architectural style for web services by listing its six defining characteristics:

Client-Server
> There must be a clear separation between the clients and the server.

Stateless
> A client request must contain all the information that is necessary to carry it out. The server must not store any state about the client that persists from one request to the next.

Cache

Responses from the server can be labeled as cacheable or noncacheable so that clients (or intermediaries between clients and servers) can use a cache for optimization purposes.

Uniform Interface

The protocol by which clients access server resources must be consistent, well defined, and standardized. The commonly used uniform interface of REST web services is the HTTP protocol.

Layered System

Proxy servers, caches, or gateways can be inserted between clients and servers as necessary to improve performance, reliability, and scalability.

Code-on-Demand

Clients can optionally download code from the server to execute in their context.

Resources Are Everything

The concept of *resources* is core to the REST architectural style. In this context, a resource is an item of interest in the domain of the application. For example, in the blogging application, users, blog posts, and comments are all resources.

Each resource must have a unique URL that represents it. Continuing with the blogging example, a blog post could be represented by the URL */api/posts/12345*, where *12345* is a unique identifier for the post such as the post's database primary key. The format or contents of the URL do not really matter; all that matters is that each resource URL uniquely identifies a resource.

A collection of all the resources in a class also has an assigned URL. The URL for the collection of blog posts could be */api/posts/* and the URL for the collection of all comments could be */api/comments/*.

An API can also define collection URLs that represent logical subsets of all the resources in a class. For example, the collection of all comments in blog post 12345 could be represented by the URL */api/posts/12345/comments/*. It is a common practice to define URLs that represent collections of resources with a trailing slash, as this gives them a "folder" representation.

 Be aware that Flask applies special treatment to routes that end with a slash. If a client requests a URL without a trailing slash and the only matching route has a slash at the end, then Flask will automatically respond with a redirect to the trailing slash URL. No redirects are issued for the reverse case.

Request Methods

The client application sends requests to the server at the established resource URLs and uses the request *method* to indicate the desired operation. To obtain the list of available blog posts in the blogging API the client would send a GET request to *http://www.example.com/api/posts/*, and to insert a new blog post it would send a POST request to the same URL, with the contents of the blog post in the request body. To retrieve blog post 12345 the client would send a GET request to *http://www.example.com/api/posts/12345*. Table 14-1 lists the request methods that are commonly used in RESTful APIs with their meanings.

Table 14-1. HTTP request methods in RESTful APIs

Request method	Target	Description	HTTP status code
GET	Individual resource URL	Obtain the resource.	200
GET	Resource collection URL	Obtain the collection of resources (or one page from it if the server implements pagination).	200
POST	Resource collection URL	Create a new resource and add it to the collection. The server chooses the URL of the new resource and returns it in a Location header in the response.	201
PUT	Individual resource URL	Modify an existing resource. Alternatively this method can also be used to create a new resource when the client can choose the resource URL.	200
DELETE	Individual resource URL	Delete a resource.	200
DELETE	Resource collection URL	Delete all resources in the collection.	200

 The REST architecture does not require that all methods be implemented for a resource. If the client invokes a method that is not supported for a given resource, then a response with the 405 status code for "Method Not Allowed" should be returned. Flask handles this error automatically.

Request and Response Bodies

Resources are sent back and forth between client and server in the bodies of requests and responses, but REST does not specify the format to use to encode resources. The Content-Type header in requests and responses is used to indicate the format in which a resource is encoded in the body. The standard content negotiation mechanisms in the HTTP protocol can be used between client and server to agree on a format that both support.

The two formats commonly used with RESTful web services are JavaScript Object Notation (JSON) and Extensible Markup Language (XML). For web-based RIAs, JSON is attractive because of its close ties to JavaScript, the client-side scripting language used by web browsers. Returning to the blog example API, a blog post resource could be represented in JSON as follows:

```
{
    "url": "http://www.example.com/api/posts/12345",
    "title": "Writing RESTful APIs in Python",
    "author": "http://www.example.com/api/users/2",
    "body": "... text of the article here ...",
    "comments": "http://www.example.com/api/posts/12345/comments"
}
```

Note how the url, author, and comments fields in the blog post above are fully qualified resource URLs. This is important because these URLs allow the client to discover new resources.

In a well-designed RESTful API, the client just knows a short list of top-level resource URLs and then discovers the rest from links included in responses, similar to how you can discover new web pages while browsing the Web by clicking on links that appear in pages that you know.

Versioning

In a traditional server-centric web application, the server has full control of the application. When an application is updated, installing the new version in the server is enough to update all users because even the parts of the application that run in the user's web browser are downloaded from the server.

The situation with RIAs and web services is more complicated, because often clients are developed independently of the server—maybe even by different people. Consider the case of an application where the RESTful web service is used by a variety of clients including web browsers and native smartphone clients. The web browser client can be updated in the server at any time, but the smartphone apps cannot be updated by force; the smartphone owner needs to allow the update to happen. Even if the smartphone owner is willing to update, it is not possible to time the deployment of the updated smartphone applications to all the app stores to coincide exactly with the deployment of the new server.

For these reasons, web services need to be more tolerant than regular web applications and be able to work with old versions of its clients. A common way to address this problem is to *version* the URLs handled by the web service. For example, the first release of the blogging web service could expose the collection of blog posts at */api/v1.0/posts/*.

Including the web service version in the URL helps keeps old and new features organized so that the server can provide new features to new clients while continuing to support old clients. An update to the blogging service could change the JSON format of blog posts and now expose blog posts as *\/api\/v1.1\/posts\/*, while keeping the older JSON format for clients that connect to *\/api\/v1.0\/posts\/*. For a period of time, the server handles all the URLs in their *v1.1* and *v1.0* variations.

Although supporting multiple versions of the server can become a maintenance burden, there are situations in which this is the only way to allow the application to grow without causing problems to existing deployments.

RESTful Web Services with Flask

Flask makes it very easy to create RESTful web services. The familiar route() decorator along with its methods optional argument can be used to declare the routes that handle the resource URLs exposed by the service. Working with JSON data is also simple, as JSON data included with a request is automatically exposed as a request.json Python dictionary and a response that needs to contain JSON can be easily generated from a Python dictionary using Flask's jsonify() helper function.

The following sections show how Flasky can be extended with a RESTful web service that gives clients access to blog posts and related resources.

Creating an API Blueprint

The routes associated with a RESTful API form a self-contained subset of the application, so putting them in their own blueprint is the best way to keep them well organized. The general structure of the API blueprint within the application is shown in Example 14-1.

Example 14-1. API blueprint structure

```
|-flasky
  |-app/
    |-api_1_0
      |-__init__.py
      |-user.py
      |-post.py
      |-comment.py
      |-authentication.py
      |-errors.py
      |-decorators.py
```

Note how the package used for the API includes a version number in its name. When a backward-incompatible version of the API needs to be introduced, it can be added as another package with a different version number and both APIs can be served at the same time.

This API blueprint implements each resource in a separate module. Modules to take care of authentication, error handling, and to provide custom decorators are also included. The blueprint constructor is shown in Example 14-2.

Example 14-2. app/api_1_0/__init__.py: API blueprint constructor

```
from flask import Blueprint

api = Blueprint('api', __name__)

from . import authentication, posts, users, comments, errors
```

The registration of the API blueprint is shown in Example 14-3.

Example 14-3. app/_init_.py: API blueprint registration

```
def create_app(config_name):
    # ...
    from .api_1_0 import api as api_1_0_blueprint
    app.register_blueprint(api_1_0_blueprint, url_prefix='/api/v1.0')
    # ...
```

Error Handling

A RESTful web service informs the client of the status of a request by sending the appropriate HTTP status code in the response plus any additional information in the response body. The typical status codes that a client can expect to see from a web service are listed in Table 14-2.

Table 14-2. HTTP response status codes typically returned by APIs

HTTP status code	Name	Description
200	OK	The request was completed successfully.
201	Created	The request was completed successfully and a new resource was created as a result.
400	Bad request	The request is invalid or inconsistent.
401	Unauthorized	The request does not include authentication information.
403	Forbidden	The authentication credentials sent with the request are insufficient for the request.
404	Not found	The resource referenced in the URL was not found.
405	Method not allowed	The request method requested is not supported for the given resource.
500	Internal server error	An unexpected error has occurred while processing the request.

The handling of status codes 404 and 500 presents a small complication, in that these errors are generated by Flask on its own and will usually return an HTML response, which is likely to confuse an API client.

One way to generate appropriate responses for all clients is to make the error handlers adapt their responses based on the format requested by the client, a technique called *content negotiation*. Example 14-4 shows an improved 404 error handler that responds with JSON to web service clients and with HTML to others. The 500 error handler is written in a similar way.

Example 14-4. app/main/errors.py: Error handlers with HTTP content negotiation

```
@main.app_errorhandler(404)
def page_not_found(e):
    if request.accept_mimetypes.accept_json and \
            not request.accept_mimetypes.accept_html:
        response = jsonify({'error': 'not found'})
        response.status_code = 404
        return response
    return render_template('404.html'), 404
```

This new version of the error handler checks the Accept request header, which Werkzeug decodes into request.accept_mimetypes, to determine what format the client wants the response in. Browsers generally do not specify any restrictions on response formats, so the JSON response is generated only for clients that accept JSON and do not accept HTML.

The remaining status codes are generated explicitly by the web service, so they can be implemented as helper functions inside the blueprint in the *errors.py* module. Example 14-5 shows the implementation of the 403 error; the others are similar.

Example 14-5. app/api/errors.py: API error handler for status code 403

```
def forbidden(message):
    response = jsonify({'error': 'forbidden', 'message': message})
    response.status_code = 403
    return response
```

Now view functions in the web service can invoke these auxiliary functions to generate error responses.

User Authentication with Flask-HTTPAuth

Web services, like regular web applications, need to protect information and ensure that it is not given to unauthorized parties. For this reason, RIAs must ask their users for login credentials and pass them to the server for verification.

It was mentioned earlier that one of the characteristics of RESTful web services is that they are *stateless*, which means that the server is not allowed to "remember" anything about the client between requests. Clients need to provide all the information necessary to carry out a request in the request itself, so all requests must include user credentials.

The current login functionality implemented with the help of Flask-Login stores data in the user session, which Flask stores by default in a client-side cookie, so the server does not store any user-related information; it asks the client to store it instead. It would appear that this implementation complies with the stateless requirement of REST, but the use of cookies in RESTful web services falls into a gray area, as it can be cumbersome for clients that are not web browsers to implement them. For that reason, it is generally seen as a bad design choice to use them.

The stateless requirement of REST may seem overly strict, but it is not arbitrary. Stateless servers can *scale* very easily. When servers store information about clients, it is necessary to have a shared cache accessible to all servers to ensure that the same server always gets requests from a given client. Both are complex problems to solve.

Because the RESTful architecture is based on the HTTP protocol, *HTTP authentication* is the preferred method used to send credentials, either in its Basic or Digest flavors. With HTTP authentication, user credentials are included in an `Authorization` header with all requests.

The HTTP authentication protocol is simple enough that it can be implemented directly, but the Flask-HTTPAuth extension provides a convenient wrapper that hides the protocol details in a decorator similar to Flask-Login's `login_required`.

Flask-HTTPAuth is installed with pip:

```
(venv) $ pip install flask-httpauth
```

To initialize the extension for HTTP Basic authentication, an object of class `HTTPBasicAuth` must be created. Like Flask-Login, Flask-HTTPAuth makes no assumptions about the procedure required to verify user credentials, so this information is given in a callback function. Example 14-6 shows how the extension is initialized and provided with a verification callback.

Example 14-6. app/api_1_0/authentication.py: Flask-HTTPAuth initialization

```python
from flask.ext.httpauth import HTTPBasicAuth
auth = HTTPBasicAuth()

@auth.verify_password
def verify_password(email, password):
    if email == '':
        g.current_user = AnonymousUser()
        return True
    user = User.query.filter_by(email = email).first()
    if not user:
        return False
    g.current_user = user
    return user.verify_password(password)
```

Because this type of user authentication will be used only in the API blueprint, the Flask-HTTPAuth extension is initialized in the blueprint package, and not in the application package like other extensions.

The email and password are verified using the existing support in the User model. The verification callback returns True when the login is valid or False otherwise. Anonymous logins are supported, for which the client must send a blank email field.

The authentication callback saves the authenticated user in Flask's g global object so that the view function can access it later. Note that when an anonymous login is received, the function returns True and saves an instance of the AnonymousUser class used with Flask-Login into g.current_user.

 Because user credentials are being exchanged with every request, it is extremely important that the API routes are exposed over secure HTTP so that all requests and responses are encrypted.

When the authentication credentials are invalid, the server returns a 401 error to the client. Flask-HTTPAuth generates a response with this status code by default, but to ensure that the response is consistent with other errors returned by the API, the error response can be customized as shown in Example 14-7.

Example 14-7. _app/api_1_0/authentication.py: Flask-HTTPAuth error handler

```
@auth.error_handler
def auth_error():
    return unauthorized('Invalid credentials')
```

To protect a route, the auth.login_required decorator is used:

```
@api.route('/posts/')
@auth.login_required
def get_posts():
    pass
```

But since all the routes in the blueprint need to be protected in the same way, the login_required decorator can be included once in a before_request handler for the blueprint, as shown in Example 14-8.

Example 14-8. app/api_1_0/authentication.py: before_request handler with authentication

```
from .errors import forbidden_error

@api.before_request
@auth.login_required
def before_request():
```

```
if not g.current_user.is_anonymous and \
        not g.current_user.confirmed:
    return forbidden('Unconfirmed account')
```

Now the authentication checks will be done automatically for all the routes in the blueprint. As an additional check, the `before_request` handler also rejects authenticated users who have not confirmed their accounts.

Token-Based Authentication

Clients must send authentication credentials with every request. To avoid having to constantly transfer sensitive information, a token-based authentication solution can be offered.

In token-based authentication, the client sends the login credentials to a special URL that generates authentication tokens. Once the client has a token it can use it in place of the login credentials to authenticate requests. For security reasons, tokens are issued with an associated expiration. When a token expires, the client must reauthenticate to get a new one. The risk of a token getting in the wrong hands is limited due to its short lifespan. Example 14-9 shows the two new methods added to the `User` model that support generation and verification of authentication tokens using itsdangerous.

Example 14-9. app/models.py: Token-based authentication support

```
class User(db.Model):
    # ...
    def generate_auth_token(self, expiration):
        s = Serializer(current_app.config['SECRET_KEY'],
                       expires_in=expiration)
        return s.dumps({'id': self.id})

    @staticmethod
    def verify_auth_token(token):
        s = Serializer(current_app.config['SECRET_KEY'])
        try:
            data = s.loads(token)
        except:
            return None
        return User.query.get(data['id'])
```

The `generate_auth_token()` method returns a signed token that encodes the user's `id` field. An expiration time given in seconds is also used. The `verify_auth_token()` method takes a token and, if found valid, it returns the user stored in it. This is a static method, as the user will be known only after the token is decoded.

To authenticate requests that come with a token, the `verify_password` callback for Flask-HTTPAuth must be modified to accept tokens as well as regular credentials. The updated callback is shown in Example 14-10.

Example 14-10. app/api_1_0/authentication.py: Improved authentication verification with token support

```
@auth.verify_password
def verify_password(email_or_token, password):
    if email_or_token == '':
        g.current_user = AnonymousUser()
        return True
    if password == '':
        g.current_user = User.verify_auth_token(email_or_token)
        g.token_used = True
        return g.current_user is not None
    user = User.query.filter_by(email=email_or_token).first()
    if not user:
        return False
    g.current_user = user
    g.token_used = False
    return user.verify_password(password)
```

In this new version, the first authentication argument can be the email address or an authentication token. If this field is blank, an anonymous user is assumed, as before. If the password is blank, then the email_or_token field is assumed to be a token and validated as such. If both fields are nonempty then regular email and password authentication is assumed. With this implementation, token-based authentication is optional; it is up to each client to use it or not. To give view functions the ability to distinguish between the two authentication methods a g.token_used variable is added.

The route that returns authentication tokens to the client is also added to the API blueprint. The implementation is shown in Example 14-11.

Example 14-11. app/api_1_0/authentication.py: Authentication token generation

```
@api.route('/token')
def get_token():
    if g.current_user.is_anonymous() or g.token_used:
        return unauthorized('Invalid credentials')
    return jsonify({'token': g.current_user.generate_auth_token(
        expiration=3600), 'expiration': 3600})
```

Since this route is in the blueprint, the authentication mechanisms added to the before_request handler also apply to it. To prevent clients from using an old token to request a new one, the g.token_used variable is checked, and in that way requests authenticated with a token can be rejected. The function returns a token in the JSON response with a validity period of one hour. The period is also included in the JSON response.

Serializing Resources to and from JSON

A frequent need when writing a web service is to convert internal representation of resources to and from JSON, which is the transport format used in HTTP requests and responses. Example 14-12 shows a new `to_json()` method added to the `Post` class.

Example 14-12. app/models.py: Convert a post to a JSON serializable dictionary

```python
class Post(db.Model):
    # ...
    def to_json(self):
        json_post = {
            'url': url_for('api.get_post', id=self.id, _external=True),
            'body': self.body,
            'body_html': self.body_html,
            'timestamp': self.timestamp,
            'author': url_for('api.get_user', id=self.author_id,
                              _external=True),
            'comments': url_for('api.get_post_comments', id=self.id,
                                _external=True)
            'comment_count': self.comments.count()
        }
        return json_post
```

The `url`, `author`, and `comments` fields need to return the URLs for the respective resources, so these are generated with `url_for()` calls to routes that will be defined in the API blueprint. Note that `_external=True` is added to all `url_for()` calls so that fully qualified URLs are returned instead of the relative URLs that are typically used within the context of a traditional web application.

This example also shows how it is possible to return "made-up" attributes in the representation of a resource. The `comment_count` field returns the number of comments that exist for the blog post. Although this is not a real attribute of the model, it is included in the resource representation as a convenience to the client.

The `to_json()` method for `User` models can be constructed in a similar way to `Post`. This method is shown in Example 14-13.

Example 14-13. app/models.py: Convert a user to a JSON serializable dictionary

```python
class User(UserMixin, db.Model):
    # ...
    def to_json(self):
        json_user = {
            'url': url_for('api.get_post', id=self.id, _external=True),
            'username': self.username,
            'member_since': self.member_since,
            'last_seen': self.last_seen,
            'posts': url_for('api.get_user_posts', id=self.id, _external=True),
            'followed_posts': url_for('api.get_user_followed_posts',
                                      id=self.id, _external=True),
```

```
        'post_count': self.posts.count()
    }
    return json_user
```

Note how in this method some of the attributes of the user, such as email and role, are omitted from the response for privacy reasons. This example again demonstrates that the representation of a resource offered to clients does not need to be identical to the internal representation of the corresponding database model.

Converting a JSON structure to a model presents the challenge that some of the data coming from the client might be invalid, wrong, or unnecessary. Example 14-14 shows the method that creates a Post model from JSON.

Example 14-14. app/models.py: Create a blog post from JSON

```
from app.exceptions import ValidationError

class Post(db.Model):
    # ...
    @staticmethod
    def from_json(json_post):
        body = json_post.get('body')
        if body is None or body == '':
            raise ValidationError('post does not have a body')
        return Post(body=body)
```

As you can see, this implementation chooses to only use the body attribute from the JSON dictionary. The body_html attribute is ignored since the server-side Markdown rendering is automatically triggered by a SQLAlchemy event whenever the body attribute is modified. The timestamp attribute does not need to be given, unless the client is allowed to backdate posts, which is not a feature of this application. The author field is not used because the client has no authority to select the author of a blog post; the only possible value for the author field is that of the authenticated user. The comments and comment_count attributes are automatically generated from a database relationship, so there is no useful information in them that is needed to create a model. Finally, the url field is ignored because in this implementation the resource URLs are defined by the server, not the client.

Note how error checking is done. If the body field is missing or empty then a ValidationError exception is raised. Throwing an exception is in this case the appropriate way to deal with the error because this method does not have enough knowledge to properly handle the condition. The exception effectively passes the error up to the caller, enabling higher level code to do the error handling. The ValidationError class is implemented as a simple subclass of Python's ValueError. This implementation is shown in Example 14-15.

Example 14-15. app/exceptions.py: ValidationError exception

```
class ValidationError(ValueError):
    pass
```

The application now needs to handle this exception by providing the appropriate response to the client. To avoid having to add exception catching code in view functions, a global exception handler can be installed. A handler for the ValidationError exception is shown in Example 14-16.

Example 14-16. app/api_1_0/errors.py: API error handler for ValidationError exceptions

```
@api.errorhandler(ValidationError)
def validation_error(e):
    return bad_request(e.args[0])
```

The errorhandler decorator is the same one that is used to register handlers for HTTP status codes, but in this usage it takes an Exception class as argument. The decorated function will be invoked any time an exception of the given class is raised. Note that the decorator is obtained from the API blueprint, so this handler will be invoked only when the exception is raised while a route from the blueprint is being processed.

Using this technique, the code in view functions can be written very cleanly and concisely, without the need to include error checking. For example:

```
@api.route('/posts/', methods=['POST'])
def new_post():
    post = Post.from_json(request.json)
    post.author = g.current_user
    db.session.add(post)
    db.session.commit()
    return jsonify(post.to_json())
```

Implementing Resource Endpoints

What remains is to implement the routes that handle the different resources. The GET requests are typically the easiest because they just return information and don't need to make any changes. Example 14-17 shows the two GET handlers for blog posts.

Example 14-17. app/api_1_0/posts.py: GET resource handlers for posts

```
@api.route('/posts/')
@auth.login_required
def get_posts():
    posts = Post.query.all()
    return jsonify({ 'posts': [post.to_json() for post in posts] })

@api.route('/posts/<int:id>')
@auth.login_required
```

```
def get_post(id):
    post = Post.query.get_or_404(id)
    return jsonify(post.to_json())
```

The first route handles the request of the collection of posts. This function uses a list comprehension to generate the JSON version of all the posts. The second route returns a single blog post and responds with a code 404 error when the given id is not found in the database.

 The handler for 404 errors is at the application level, but it will provide a JSON response if the client requests that format. If a response
customized to the web service is desired, the 404 error handler can
be overridden in the blueprint.

The POST handler for blog post resources inserts a new blog post in the database. This route is shown in Example 14-18.

Example 14-18. app/api_1_0/posts.py: POST resource handler for posts

```
@api.route('/posts/', methods=['POST'])
@permission_required(Permission.WRITE_ARTICLES)
def new_post():
    post = Post.from_json(request.json)
    post.author = g.current_user
    db.session.add(post)
    db.session.commit()
    return jsonify(post.to_json()), 201, \
            {'Location': url_for('api.get_post', id=post.id, _external=True)}
```

This view function is wrapped in a permission_required decorator (shown in an up-coming example) that ensures that the authenticated user has the permission to write blog posts. The actual creation of the blog post is straightforward due to the error handling support that was implemented previously. A blog post is created from the JSON data and its author is explicitly assigned as the authenticated user. After the model is written to the database, a 201 status code is returned and a Location header is added with the URL of the newly created resource.

Note that for convenience to the client, the body of the response includes the new re-source. This will save the client from having to issue a GET resource for it immediately after creating the resource.

The permission_required decorator used to prevent unauthorized users from creating new blog posts is similar to the one used in the application but is customized for the API blueprint. The implementation is shown in Example 14-19.

Example 14-19. app/api_1_0/decorators.py: permission_required decorator

```
def permission_required(permission):
    def decorator(f):
        @wraps(f)
        def decorated_function(*args, **kwargs):
            if not g.current_user.can(permission):
                return forbidden('Insufficient permissions')
            return f(*args, **kwargs)
        return decorated_function
    return decorator
```

The PUT handler for blog posts, used for editing existing resources, is shown in Example 14-20.

Example 14-20. app/api_1_0/posts.py: PUT resource handler for posts

```
@api.route('/posts/<int:id>', methods=['PUT'])
@permission_required(Permission.WRITE_ARTICLES)
def edit_post(id):
    post = Post.query.get_or_404(id)
    if g.current_user != post.author and \
            not g.current_user.can(Permission.ADMINISTER):
        return forbidden('Insufficient permissions')
    post.body = request.json.get('body', post.body)
    db.session.add(post)
    return jsonify(post.to_json())
```

The permission checks are more complex in this case. The standard check for permission to write blog posts is done with the decorator, but to allow a user to edit a blog post the function must also ensure that the user is the author of the post or else is an administrator. This check is added explicitly to the view function. If this check had to be added in many view functions, building a decorator for it would be a good way to avoid code repetition.

Since the application does not allow deletion of posts, the handler for the DELETE request method does not need to be implemented.

The resource handlers for users and comments are implemented in a similar way. Table 14-3 lists the set of resources implemented for this application. The complete implementation is available for you to study in the GitHub repository (*http://bit.ly/ flasky-git*).

Table 14-3. Flasky API resources

Resource URL	Methods	Description
/users/<int:id>	GET	A user
/users/<int:id>/posts/	GET	The blog posts written by a user
/users/<int:id>/timeline/	GET	The blog posts followed by a user

Resource URL	Methods	Description
/posts/	GET, POST	All the blog posts
/posts/<int:id>	GET, PUT	A blog post
/posts/<int:id/>comments/	GET, POST	The comments on a blog post
/comments/	GET	All the comments
/comments/<int:id>	GET	A comment

Note that the resources that were implemented enable a client to offer a subset of the functionality that is available through the web application. The list of supported resources could be expanded if necessary, such as to expose followers, to enable comment moderation, and to implement any other features that a client might need.

Pagination of Large Resource Collections

The GET requests that return a collection of resources can be extremely expensive and difficult to manage for very large collections. Like web applications, web services can choose to paginate collections.

Example 14-21 shows a possible implementation of pagination for the list of blog posts.

Example 14-21. app/api_1_0/posts.py: Post pagination

```
@api.route('/posts/')
def get_posts():
    page = request.args.get('page', 1, type=int)
    pagination = Post.query.paginate(
        page, per_page=current_app.config['FLASKY_POSTS_PER_PAGE'],
        error_out=False)
    posts = pagination.items
    prev = None
    if pagination.has_prev:
        prev = url_for('api.get_posts', page=page-1, _external=True)
    next = None
    if pagination.has_next:
        next = url_for('api.get_posts', page=page+1, _external=True)
    return jsonify({
        'posts': [post.to_json() for post in posts],
        'prev': prev,
        'next': next,
        'count': pagination.total
    })
```

The posts field in the JSON response contains the data items as before, but now it is just a portion of the complete set. The prev and next items contain the resource URLs for the previous and following pages, when available. The count value is the total number of items in the collection.

This technique can be applied to all the routes that return collections.

 If you have cloned the application's Git repository on GitHub, you can run `git checkout 14a` to check out this version of the application. To ensure that you have all the dependencies installed, also run `pip install -r requirements/dev.txt`.

Testing Web Services with HTTPie

To test a web service, an HTTP client must be used. The two most used clients for testing web services from the command line are *curl* and *HTTPie*. The latter has a much more concise and readable command line. HTTPie is installed with pip:

```
(venv) $ pip install httpie
```

A GET request can be issued as follows:

```
(venv) $ http --json --auth <email>:<password> GET \
> http://127.0.0.1:5000/api/v1.0/posts
HTTP/1.0 200 OK
Content-Length: 7018
Content-Type: application/json
Date: Sun, 22 Dec 2013 08:11:24 GMT
Server: Werkzeug/0.9.4 Python/2.7.3

{
    "posts": [
        ...
    ],
    "prev": null
    "next": "http://127.0.0.1:5000/api/v1.0/posts/?page=2",
    "count": 150
}
```

Note the pagination links included in the response. Since this is the first page, a previous page is not defined, but a URL to obtain the next page and a total count were returned.

The same request can be issued by an anonymous user by sending an empty email and password:

```
(venv) $ http --json --auth : GET http://127.0.0.1:5000/api/v1.0/posts/
```

The following command sends a POST request to add a new blog post:

```
(venv) $ http --auth <email>:<password> --json POST \
> http://127.0.0.1:5000/api/v1.0/posts/ \
> "body=I'm adding a post from the *command line*."
HTTP/1.0 201 CREATED
Content-Length: 360
Content-Type: application/json
Date: Sun, 22 Dec 2013 08:30:27 GMT
```

```
Location: http://127.0.0.1:5000/api/v1.0/posts/111
Server: Werkzeug/0.9.4 Python/2.7.3

{
    "author": "http://127.0.0.1:5000/api/v1.0/users/1",
    "body": "I'm adding a post from the *command line*.",
    "body_html": "<p>I'm adding a post from the <em>command line</em>.</p>",
    "comments": "http://127.0.0.1:5000/api/v1.0/posts/111/comments",
    "comment_count": 0,
    "timestamp": "Sun, 22 Dec 2013 08:30:27 GMT",
    "url": "http://127.0.0.1:5000/api/v1.0/posts/111"
}
```

To use authentication tokens, a request to *api/v1.0/token* is sent:

```
(venv) $ http --auth <email>:<password> --json GET \
> http://127.0.0.1:5000/api/v1.0/token
HTTP/1.0 200 OK
Content-Length: 162
Content-Type: application/json
Date: Sat, 04 Jan 2014 08:38:47 GMT
Server: Werkzeug/0.9.4 Python/3.3.3

{
    "expiration": 3600,
    "token": "eyJpYXQiOjEzODg4MjQ3MjcsImV4cCI6MTM4ODgyODMyNywiYWxnIjoiSFMy..."
}
```

And now the returned token can be used to make calls into the API for the next hour by passing it along with an empty password field:

```
(venv) $ http --json --auth eyJpYXQ...: GET http://127.0.0.1:5000/api/v1.0/posts/
```

When the token expires, requests will be returned with a code 401 error, indicating that a new token needs to be obtained.

Congratulations! This chapter completes Part II, and with that the feature development phase of Flasky is complete. The next step is obviously to deploy it, and that brings a new set of challenges that are the subject of Part III.

## PART III

The Last Mile

## CHAPTER 15

Testing

There are two very good reasons for writing unit tests. When implementing new functionality, unit tests are used to confirm that the new code is working in the expected way. The same result can be obtained by testing manually, but of course automated tests save time and effort.

A second, more important reason is that each time the application is modified, all the unit tests built around it can be executed to ensure that there are no *regressions* in the existing code; in other words, that the new changes did not affect the way the older code works.

Unit tests have been a part of Flasky since the very beginning, with tests designed to exercise specific features of the application implemented in the database model classes. These classes are easy to test outside of the context of a running application, so given that it takes little effort, implementing unit tests for all the features implemented in the database models is the best way to ensure at least that part of the application starts robust and stays that way.

This chapter discusses ways to improve and extend unit testing.

Obtaining Code Coverage Reports

Having a test suite is important, but it is equally important to know how good or bad it is. Code coverage tools measure how much of the application is exercised by unit tests and can provide a detailed report that indicates which parts of the application code are not being tested. This information is invaluable, because it can be used to direct the effort of writing new tests to the areas that need it most.

Python has an excellent code coverage tool appropriately called *coverage*. You can install it with pip:

```
(venv) $ pip install coverage
```

This tool comes as a command-line script that can launch any Python application with code coverage enabled, but it also provides more convenient scripting access to start the coverage engine programmatically. To have coverage metrics nicely integrated into the *manage.py* launcher script, the custom `test` command added in Chapter 7 can be expanded with a `--coverage` optional argument. The implementation of this option is shown in Example 15-1.

Example 15-1. manage.py: Coverage metrics

```python
#!/usr/bin/env python
import os
COV = None
if os.environ.get('FLASK_COVERAGE'):
    import coverage
    COV = coverage.coverage(branch=True, include='app/*')
    COV.start()

# ...

@manager.command
def test(coverage=False):
    """Run the unit tests."""
    if coverage and not os.environ.get('FLASK_COVERAGE'):
        import sys
        os.environ['FLASK_COVERAGE'] = '1'
        os.execvp(sys.executable, [sys.executable] + sys.argv)
    import unittest
    tests = unittest.TestLoader().discover('tests')
    unittest.TextTestRunner(verbosity=2).run(tests)
    if COV:
        COV.stop()
        COV.save()
        print('Coverage Summary:')
        COV.report()
        basedir = os.path.abspath(os.path.dirname(__file__))
        covdir = os.path.join(basedir, 'tmp/coverage')
        COV.html_report(directory=covdir)
        print('HTML version: file://%s/index.html' % covdir)
        COV.erase()

# ...
```

Flask-Script makes it very easy to define custom commands. To add a Boolean option to the `test` command, add a Boolean argument to the `test()` function. Flask-Script derives the name of the option from the argument name and passes `True` or `False` to the function accordingly.

But integrating code coverage with the *manage.py* script presents a small problem. By the time the `--coverage` option is received in the `test()` function, it is already too late to turn on coverage metrics; by that time all the code in the global scope has already executed. To get accurate metrics, the script restarts itself after setting the `FLASK_COVERAGE` environment variable. In the second run, the top of the script finds that the environment variable is set and turns on coverage from the start.

The `coverage.coverage()` function starts the coverage engine. The `branch=True` option enables branch coverage analysis, which, in addition to tracking which lines of code execute, checks whether for every conditional both the `True` and `False` cases have executed. The `include` option is used to limit coverage analysis to the files that are inside the application package, which is the only code that needs to be measured. Without the `include` option, all the extensions installed in the virtual environment and the code for the tests itself would be included in the coverage reports—and that would add a lot of noise to the report.

After all the tests have executed, the `text()` function writes a report to the console and also writes a nicer HTML report to disk. The HTML version is very good for displaying coverage visually because it shows the source code lines color-coded according to their use.

 If you have cloned the application's Git repository on GitHub, you can run `git checkout 15a` to check out this version of the application. To ensure that you have all the dependencies installed, also run `pip install -r requirements/dev.txt`.

An example of the text-based report follows:

```
(venv) $ python manage.py test --coverage
...
.------------------------------------------------------------------
Ran 19 tests in 50.609s

OK
Coverage Summary:
Name                         Stmts  Miss Branch BrMiss  Cover   Missing
...
.------------------------------------------------------------------
app/__init__                    33     0      0      0   100%
app/api_1_0/__init__             3     0      0      0   100%
app/api_1_0/authentication      30    19     11     11    27%
app/api_1_0/comments            40    30     12     12    19%
app/api_1_0/decorators          11     3      2      2    62%
app/api_1_0/errors              17    10      0      0    41%
app/api_1_0/posts               35    23      9      9    27%
app/api_1_0/users               30    24     12     12    14%
app/auth/__init__                3     0      0      0   100%
app/auth/forms                  45     8      8      8    70%
app/auth/views                 109    84     41     41    17%
app/decorators                  14     3      2      2    69%
```

```
app/email                           15     9     0     0    40%
app/exceptions                       2     0     0     0   100%
app/main/__init__                    6     1     0     0    83%
app/main/errors                     20    15     9     9    17%
app/main/forms                      39     7     8     8    68%
app/main/views                     169   131    36    36    19%
app/models                         243    62    44    17    72%
-------------------------------------------------------------------
TOTAL                              864   429   194   167    44%
HTML version: file:///home/flask/flasky/tmp/coverage/index.html
```

The report shows an overall coverage of 44%, which is not terrible, but isn't very good either. The model classes, which have received all the unit testing attention so far, constitute a total of 243 statements, of which 72% are covered in tests. Obviously the *views.py* files in the main and auth blueprints and the routes in the api_1_0 blueprint all have very low coverage, since these are not exercised in any of the existing unit tests.

Armed with this report, it is easy to determine which tests need to be added to the test suite to improve coverage, but unfortunately not all parts of the application can be tested as easily as the database models. The next two sections discuss more advanced testing strategies that can be applied to view functions, forms, and templates.

Note that the contents of the *Missing* column have been omitted in the example report to improve the formatting. This column indicates the source code lines that were missed by the tests as a long list of line number ranges.

The Flask Test Client

Some portions of the application code rely heavily on the environment that is created by a running application. For example, you can't simply invoke the code in a view function to test it, as the function may need to access Flask context globals such as request or session, it may be expecting form data in a POST request, and some view functions may also require a logged-in user. In short, view functions can run only within the context of a request and a running application.

Flask comes equipped with a *test client* to try to address this problem, at least partially. The test client replicates the environment that exists when an application is running inside a web server, allowing tests to act as clients and send requests.

The view functions do not see any major differences when executed under the test client; requests are received and routed to the appropriate view functions, from which responses are generated and returned. After a view function executes, its response is passed to the test, which can check it for correctness.

Testing Web Applications

Example 15-2 shows a unit testing framework that uses the test client.

Example 15-2. tests/test_client.py: Framework for tests using the Flask test client

```
import unittest
from app import create_app, db
from app.models import User, Role

class FlaskClientTestCase(unittest.TestCase):
    def setUp(self):
        self.app = create_app('testing')
        self.app_context = self.app.app_context()
        self.app_context.push()
        db.create_all()
        Role.insert_roles()
        self.client = self.app.test_client(use_cookies=True)

    def tearDown(self):
        db.session.remove()
        db.drop_all()
        self.app_context.pop()

    def test_home_page(self):
        response = self.client.get(url_for('main.index'))
        self.assertTrue('Stranger' in response.get_data(as_text=True))
```

The self.client instance variable added to the test case is the Flask test client object. This object exposes methods that issue requests into the application. When the test client is created with the use_cookies option enabled, it will accept and send cookies in the same way browsers do, so functionality that relies on cookies to recall context between requests can be used. In particular, this approach enables the use of user sessions, so it is necessary to log users in and out.

The test_home_page() test is a simple example of what the test client can do. In this example, a request for the home page is issued. The return value of the get() method of the test client is a Flask Response object, containing the response returned by the invoked view function. To check whether the test was successful, the body of the response, obtained from response.get_data(), is searched for the word "Stranger", which is part of the "Hello, Stranger!" greeting shown to anonymous users. Note that get_data() returns the response body as a byte array by default; passing as_text=True returns a Unicode string that is much easier to work with.

The test client can also send POST requests that include form data using the post() method, but submitting forms presents a small complication. The forms generated by Flask-WTF have a hidden field with a CSRF token that needs to be submitted along with the form. To replicate this functionality, a test would need to request the page that includes the form, then parse the HTML text returned in the response and extract the token so that it can then send the token with the form data. To avoid the hassle of dealing with CSRF tokens in tests, it is better to disable CSRF protection in the testing config-uration. This is as shown in Example 15-3.

Example 15-3. config.py: Disable CSRF protection in the testing configuration

```
class TestingConfig(Config):
    #...
    WTF_CSRF_ENABLED = False
```

Example 15-4 shows a more advanced unit test that simulates a new user registering an account, logging in, confirming the account with a confirmation token, and finally log-ging out.

Example 15-4. tests/test_client.py: Simulation of a new user workflow with the Flask test client

```
class FlaskClientTestCase(unittest.TestCase):
    # ...
    def test_register_and_login(self):
        # register a new account
        response = self.client.post(url_for('auth.register'), data={
            'email': 'john@example.com',
            'username': 'john',
            'password': 'cat',
            'password2': 'cat'
        })
        self.assertTrue(response.status_code == 302)

        # login with the new account
        response = self.client.post(url_for('auth.login'), data={
            'email': 'john@example.com',
            'password': 'cat'
        }, follow_redirects=True)
        data = response.get_data(as_text=True)
        self.assertTrue(re.search('Hello,\s+john!', data))
        self.assertTrue('You have not confirmed your account yet' in data)

        # send a confirmation token
        user = User.query.filter_by(email='john@example.com').first()
        token = user.generate_confirmation_token()
        response = self.client.get(url_for('auth.confirm', token=token),
                                   follow_redirects=True)
        data = response.get_data(as_text=True)
        self.assertTrue('You have confirmed your account' in data)

        # log out
        response = self.client.get(url_for('auth.logout'),
                                   follow_redirects=True)
        data = response.get_data(as_text=True)
        self.assertTrue('You have been logged out' in data)
```

The test begins with a form submission to the registration route. The `data` argument to `post()` is a dictionary with the form fields, which must exactly match the field names defined in the form. Since CSRF protection is now disabled in the testing configuration, there is no need to send the CSRF token with the form.

The *auth/register* route can respond in two ways. If the registration data is valid, a redirect sends the user to the login page. In the case of an invalid registration, the response renders the page with the registration form again, including any appropriate error messages. To validate that the registration was accepted, the test checks that the status code of the response is 302, which is the code for a redirect.

The second section of the test issues a login to the application using the email and password just registered. This is done with a `POST` request to the *auth/login* route. This time a `follow_redirects=True` argument is included in the `post()` call to make the test client work like a browser and automatically issue a `GET` request for the redirected URL. With this option, status code 302 will not be returned; instead, the response from the redirected URL is returned.

A successful response to the login submission would now have a page that greets the user by the username and then indicates that the account needs to be confirmed to gain access. Two assert statements verify that this is the page, and here it is interesting to note that a search for the string `'Hello, john!'` would not work because this string is assembled from static and dynamic portions, with extra whitespace in between the parts. To avoid an error in this test due to the whitespace, a more flexible regular expression is used.

The next step is to confirm the account, which presents another small obstacle. The confirmation URL is sent to the user by email during registration, so there is no easy way to access it from the test. The solution presented in the example bypasses the token that was generated as part of the registration and generates another one directly from the `User` instance. Another possibility would have been to extract the token by parsing the email body, which Flask-Mail saves when running in a testing configuration.

With the token at hand, the third part of the test is to simulate the user clicking the confirmation token URL. This is achieved by sending a `GET` request to the confirmation URL with the token attached. The response to this request is a redirect to the home page, but once again `follow_redirects=True` was specified, so the test client requests the redirected page automatically. The response is checked for the greeting and a flashed message that informs the user that the confirmation was successful.

The final step in this test is to send a `GET` request to the logout route; to confirm that this has worked, the test searches for a flashed message in the response.

If you have cloned the application's Git repository on GitHub, you can run `git checkout 15b` to check out this version of the application.

Testing Web Services

The Flask test client can also be used to test RESTful web services. Example 15-5 shows an example unit test class with two tests.

Example 15-5. tests/test_api.py: RESTful API testing with the Flask test client

```python
class APITestCase(unittest.TestCase):
    # ...
    def get_api_headers(self, username, password):
        return {
            'Authorization':
                'Basic ' + b64encode(
                    (username + ':' + password).encode('utf-8')).decode('utf-8'),
            'Accept': 'application/json',
            'Content-Type': 'application/json'
        }

    def test_no_auth(self):
        response = self.client.get(url_for('api.get_posts'),
                                   content_type='application/json')
        self.assertTrue(response.status_code == 401)

    def test_posts(self):
        # add a user
        r = Role.query.filter_by(name='User').first()
        self.assertIsNotNone(r)
        u = User(email='john@example.com', password='cat', confirmed=True,
                 role=r)
        db.session.add(u)
        db.session.commit()

        # write a post
        response = self.client.post(
            url_for('api.new_post'),
            headers=self.get_auth_header('john@example.com', 'cat'),
            data=json.dumps({'body': 'body of the blog post'}))
        self.assertTrue(response.status_code == 201)
        url = response.headers.get('Location')
        self.assertIsNotNone(url)

        # get the new post
        response = self.client.get(
            url,
            headers=self.get_auth_header('john@example.com', 'cat'))
```

```
self.assertTrue(response.status_code == 200)
json_response = json.loads(response.data.decode('utf-8'))
self.assertTrue(json_response['url'] == url)
self.assertTrue(json_response['body'] == 'body of the *blog* post')
self.assertTrue(json_response['body_html'] ==
                    '<p>body of the <em>blog</em> post</p>')
```

The setUp() and tearDown() methods for testing the API are the same as for the regular application, but the cookie support does not need to be configured because the API does not use it. The get_api_headers() method is a helper method that returns the common headers that need to be sent with all requests. These include the authentication credentials and the MIME-type related headers. Most of the tests need to send these headers.

The test_no_auth() test is a simple test that ensures that a request that does not include authentication credentials is rejected with error code 401. The test_posts() test adds a user to the database and then uses the RESTful API to insert a blog post and then read it back. Any requests that send data in the body must encode it with json.dumps(), because the Flask test client does not automatically encode to JSON. Likewise, response bodies are also returned in JSON format and must be decoded with json.loads() before they can be inspected.

> If you have cloned the application's Git repository on GitHub, you can run git checkout 15c to check out this version of the application.

End-to-End Testing with Selenium

The Flask test client cannot fully emulate the environment of a running application. For example, any application that relies on JavaScript code running in the client browser will not work, as the JavaScript code included in the responses returned to the test will not be executed as they would be in a real web browser client.

When tests require the complete environment, there is no other choice than to use a real web browser connected to the application running under a real web server. Fortunately, most web browsers can be automated. Selenium (*http://www.seleniumhq.org/*) is a web browser automation tool that supports the most popular web browsers in the three major operating systems.

The Python interface for Selenium is installed with pip:

```
(venv) $ pip install selenium
```

Testing with Selenium requires the application to be running inside a web server that is listening for real HTTP requests. The method that will be shown in this section starts the application with the development server in a background thread while the tests run on the main thread. Under the control of the tests, Selenium launches a web browser and makes it connect to the application to perform the required operations

A problem with this approach is that after all the tests have completed, the Flask server needs to be stopped, ideally in a graceful way, so that background tasks such as the code coverage engine can cleanly complete their work. The Werkzeug web server has a shutdown option, but because the server is running isolated in its own thread, the only way to ask the server to shut down is by sending a regular HTTP request. Example 15-6 shows the implementation of a server shutdown route.

Example 15-6. _app/main/views.py: Server shutdown route

```
@main.route('/shutdown')
def server_shutdown():
    if not current_app.testing:
        abort(404)
    shutdown = request.environ.get('werkzeug.server.shutdown')
    if not shutdown:
        abort(500)
    shutdown()
    return 'Shutting down...'
```

The shutdown route will work only when the application is running in testing mode; invoking it in other configurations will fail. The actual shutdown procedure involves calling a shutdown function that Werkzeug exposes in the environment. After calling this function and returning from the request, the development web server will know that it needs to exit gracefully.

Example 15-7 shows the layout of a test case that is configured to run tests with Selenium.

Example 15-7. tests/test_selenium.py: Framework for tests using Selenium

```
from selenium import webdriver

class SeleniumTestCase(unittest.TestCase):
    client = None

    @classmethod
    def setUpClass(cls):
        # start Firefox
        try:
            cls.client = webdriver.Firefox()
        except:
            pass

        # skip these tests if the browser could not be started
        if cls.client:
            # create the application
            cls.app = create_app('testing')
            cls.app_context = cls.app.app_context()
```

```
        cls.app_context.push()

        # suppress logging to keep unittest output clean
        import logging
        logger = logging.getLogger('werkzeug')
        logger.setLevel("ERROR")

        # create the database and populate with some fake data
        db.create_all()
        Role.insert_roles()
        User.generate_fake(10)
        Post.generate_fake(10)

        # add an administrator user
        admin_role = Role.query.filter_by(permissions=0xff).first()
        admin = User(email='john@example.com',
                     username='john', password='cat',
                     role=admin_role, confirmed=True)
        db.session.add(admin)
        db.session.commit()

        # start the Flask server in a thread
        threading.Thread(target=cls.app.run).start()

    @classmethod
    def tearDownClass(cls):
        if cls.client:
            # stop the flask server and the browser
            cls.client.get('http://localhost:5000/shutdown')
            cls.client.close()

            # destroy database
            db.drop_all()
            db.session.remove()

            # remove application context
            cls.app_context.pop()

    def setUp(self):
        if not self.client:
            self.skipTest('Web browser not available')

    def tearDown(self):
        pass
```

The setUpClass() and tearDownClass() class methods are invoked before and after the tests in this class execute. The setup involves starting an instance of Firefox through Selenium's webdriver API and creating an application and a database with some initial data for tests to use. The application is started in a thread using the standard app.run() method. At the end the application receives a request to /shutdown, which causes the background thread to end. The browser is then closed and the test database removed.

Selenium supports many other web browsers besides Firefox. Consult the Selenium documentation (*http://bit.ly/sel-docs*) if you wish to use a different web browser.

The `setUp()` method that runs before each test skips tests if Selenium cannot start the web browser in the `startUpClass()` method. In Example 15-8 you can see an example test built with Selenium.

Example 15-8. tests/test_selenium.py: Example Selenium unit test

```
class SeleniumTestCase(unittest.TestCase):
    # ...

    def test_admin_home_page(self):
        # navigate to home page
        self.client.get('http://localhost:5000/')
        self.assertTrue(re.search('Hello,\s+Stranger!',
                                  self.client.page_source))

        # navigate to login page
        self.client.find_element_by_link_text('Log In').click()
        self.assertTrue('<h1>Login</h1>' in self.client.page_source)

        # login
        self.client.find_element_by_name('email').\
            send_keys('john@example.com')
        self.client.find_element_by_name('password').send_keys('cat')
        self.client.find_element_by_name('submit').click()
        self.assertTrue(re.search('Hello,\s+john!', self.client.page_source))

        # navigate to the user's profile page
        self.client.find_element_by_link_text('Profile').click()
        self.assertTrue('<h1>john</h1>' in self.client.page_source)
```

This test logs in to the application using the administrator account that was created in `setUpClass()` and then opens the profile page. Note how different the testing methodology is from the Flask test client. When testing with Selenium, tests send commands to the web browser and never interact with the application directly. The commands closely match the actions that a real user would perform with mouse or keyboard.

The test begins with a call to `get()` with the home page of the application. In the browser, this causes the URL to be entered in the address bar. To verify this step, the page source is checked for the "Hello, Stranger!" greeting.

To go to the sign-in page, the test looks for the "Log In" link using `find_element_by_link_text()` and then calls `click()` on it to trigger a real click in the browser. Selenium provides several `find_element_by...()` convenience methods that can search for elements in different ways.

To log in to the application, the test locates the email and password form fields by their names using `find_element_by_name()` and then writes text into them with `send_keys()`. The form is submitted by calling `click()` on the submit button. The personalized greeting is checked to ensure that the login was successful and the browser is now on the home page.

The final part of the test locates the "Profile" link in the navigation bar and clicks it. To verify that the profile page was loaded, the heading with the username is searched in the page source.

 If you have cloned the application's Git repository on GitHub, you can run `git checkout 15d` to check out this version of the application. This update contains a database migration, so remember to run `python manage.py db upgrade` after you check out the code. To ensure that you have all the dependencies installed, also run `pip install -r requirements/dev.txt`.

Is It Worth It?

By now you may be asking if testing using the Flask test client or Selenium is really worth the trouble. It is a valid question, and it does not have a simple answer.

Whether you like it or not, your application will be tested. If you don't test it yourself, then your users will become the unwilling testers that will be finding the bugs, and then you will have to fix bugs under pressure. Simple and focused tests like the ones that exercise database models and other parts of the application that can be executed outside of the context of an application should always be used, as they have a very low cost and ensure the proper functioning of the core pieces of application logic.

End-to-end tests of the type that the Flask test client and Selenium can carry out are sometimes necessary, but due to the increased complexity to write them, they should be used only for functionality that cannot be tested in isolation. The application code should be organized so that it is possible to push as much of the business logic as possible into database models or other auxiliary classes that are independent of the context of the application and thus can be tested easily. The code that exists in view functions should be simple and just act as a thin layer that accepts requests and invokes the corresponding actions in other classes or functions that encapsulate the application logic.

So yes, testing is absolutely worth it. But it is important to design an efficient testing strategy and write code that can take advantage of it.

## CHAPTER 16

Performance

Nobody likes slow applications. Long waits for pages to load frustrate users, so it is important to detect and correct performance problems as soon as they appear. In this chapter, two important performance aspects of web applications are considered.

Logging Slow Database Performance

When application performance slowly degenerates with time, it is likely due to slow database queries, which get worse as the size of the database grows. Optimizing database queries can be as simple as adding more indexes or as complex as adding a cache between the application and the database. The `explain` statement, available in most database query languages, shows the steps the database takes to execute a given query, often exposing inefficiencies in database or index design.

But before starting to optimize queries, it is necessary to determine which queries are the ones that are worth optimizing. During a typical request several database queries may be issued, so it is often hard to identify which of all the queries are the slow ones. Flask-SQLAlchemy has an option to record statistics about database queries issued during a request. In Example 16-1 you can see how this feature can be used to *log* queries that are slower than a configured threshold.

Example 16-1. app/main/views.py: Report slow database queries

```
from flask.ext.sqlalchemy import get_debug_queries

@main.after_app_request
def after_request(response):
    for query in get_debug_queries():
        if query.duration >= current_app.config['FLASKY_SLOW_DB_QUERY_TIME']:
            current_app.logger.warning(
                'Slow query: %s\nParameters: %s\nDuration: %fs\nContext: %s\n' %
                    (query.statement, query.parameters, query.duration,
```

```
            query.context))
    return response
```

This functionality is attached to an `after_app_request` handler, which works in a similar way to the `before_app_request` handler, but is invoked after the view function that handles the request returns. Flask passes the response object to the `after_app_request` handler in case it needs to be modified.

In this case, the `after_app_request` handler does not modify the response; it just gets the query timings recorded by Flask-SQLAlchemy and logs any of the slow ones.

The `get_debug_queries()` function returns the queries issued during the request as a list. The information provided for each query is shown in Table 16-1.

Table 16-1. Query statistics recorded by Flask-SQLAlchemy

Name	Description
statement	The SQL statement
parameters	The parameters used with the SQL statement
start_time	The time the query was issued
end_time	The time the query returned
duration	The duration of the query in seconds
context	A string that indicates the source code location where the query was issued

The `after_app_request` handler walks the list and logs any queries that lasted longer than a threshold given in the configuration. The logging is issued at the warning level. Changing the level to "error" would cause all slow query occurrences to be emailed as well.

The `get_debug_queries()` function is enabled only in debug mode by default. Unfortunately, database performance problems rarely show up during development because much smaller databases are used. For this reason, it is useful to use this option in production. Example 16-2 shows the configuration changes that are necessary to enable database query performance in production mode.

Example 16-2. config.py: Configuration for slow query reporting

```
class Config:
    # ...
    SQLALCHEMY_RECORD_QUERIES = True
    FLASKY_DB_QUERY_TIMEOUT = 0.5
    # ...
```

`SQLALCHEMY_RECORD_QUERIES` tells Flask-SQLAlchemy to enable the recording of query statistics. The slow query threshold is set to half a second. Both configuration variables were included in the base `Config` class, so they will be enabled for all configurations.

Whenever a slow query is detected, an entry will be written to Flask's application logger. To be able to store these log entries, the logger must be configured. The logging configuration largely depends on the platform that hosts the application. Some examples are shown in Chapter 17.

 If you have cloned the application's Git repository on GitHub, you can run git checkout 16a to check out this version of the application.

Source Code Profiling

Another possible source of performance problems is high CPU consumption, caused by functions that perform heavy computing. Source code profilers are useful in finding the slowest parts of an application. A profiler watches a running application and records the functions that are called and how long each takes to run. It then produces a detailed report showing the slowest functions.

 Profiling is typically done in a development environment. A source code profiler makes the application run slower because it has to observe and take notes of all that is happening. Profiling on a production system is not recommended, unless a lightweight profiler specifically designed to run on a production environment is used.

Flask's development web server, which comes from Werkzeug, can optionally enable the Python profiler for each request. Example 16-3 adds a new command-line option to the application that starts the profiler.

Example 16-3. manage.py: Run the application under the request profiler

```
@manager.command
def profile(length=25, profile_dir=None):
    """Start the application under the code profiler."""
    from werkzeug.contrib.profiler import ProfilerMiddleware
    app.wsgi_app = ProfilerMiddleware(app.wsgi_app, restrictions=[length],
                                      profile_dir=profile_dir)
    app.run()
```

 If you have cloned the application's Git repository on GitHub, you can run git checkout 16b to check out this version of the application.

When the application is started with `python manage.py profile`, the console will show the profiler statistics for each request, which will include the slowest 25 functions. The `--length` option can be used to change the number of functions shown in the report. If the `--profile-dir` option is given, the profile data for each request will be saved to a file in the given directory. The profiler data files can be used to generate more detailed reports that include a *call graph*. For more information on the Python profiler, consult the official documentation (*http://bit.ly/py-profile*).

The preparations for deployment are complete. The next chapter will give you an overview of what to expect when deploying your application.

## CHAPTER 17

Deployment

The web development server that comes bundled with Flask is not robust, secure, or efficient enough to work in a production environment. In this chapter, deployment options for Flask applications are examined.

Deployment Workflow

Regardless of the hosting method used, there are a series of tasks that must be carried out when the application is installed on a production server. The best example is the creation or update of the database tables.

Having to run these tasks manually each time the application is installed or upgraded is error prone and time consuming, so instead a command that performs all the required tasks can be added to *manage.py*.

Example 17-1 shows a deploy command implementation that is appropriate for Flasky.

Example 17-1. manage.py: deploy command

```
@manager.command
def deploy():
    """Run deployment tasks."""
    from flask.ext.migrate import upgrade
    from app.models import Role, User

    # migrate database to latest revision
    upgrade()

    # create user roles
    Role.insert_roles()

    # create self-follows for all users
    User.add_self_follows()
```

The functions invoked by this command were all created before; they are just invoked all together.

 If you have cloned the application's Git repository on GitHub, you can run `git checkout 17a` to check out this version of the application.

These functions are all designed in a way that causes no problems if they are executed multiple times. Designing update functions in this way makes it possible to run just this `deploy` command every time an installation or upgrade is done.

Logging of Errors During Production

When the application is running in debug mode, Werkzeug's interactive debugger appears whenever an error occurs. The *stack trace* of the error is displayed on the web page and it is possible to look at the source code and even evaluate expressions in the context of each stack frame using Flask's interactive web-based debugger.

The debugger is an excellent tool to debug application problems during development, but obviously it cannot be used in a production deployment. Errors that occur in production are silenced and instead the user receives a code 500 error page. But luckily, the stack traces of these errors are not completely lost, as Flask writes them to a *log file*.

During startup, Flask creates an instance of Python's `logging.Logger` class and attaches it to the application instance as `app.logger`. In debug mode, this logger writes to the console, but in production mode there are no handlers configured for it by default, so unless a handler is added logs are not stored. The changes in Example 17-2 configure a logging handler that sends the errors that occur while running in production mode to the list administrator emails configured in the `FLASKY_ADMIN` setting.

Example 17-2. config.py: Send email for application errors

```
class ProductionConfig(Config):
    # ...
    @classmethod
    def init_app(cls, app):
        Config.init_app(app)

        # email errors to the administrators
        import logging
        from logging.handlers import SMTPHandler
        credentials = None
        secure = None
        if getattr(cls, 'MAIL_USERNAME', None) is not None:
            credentials = (cls.MAIL_USERNAME, cls.MAIL_PASSWORD)
```

```
        if getattr(cls, 'MAIL_USE_TLS', None):
            secure = ()
    mail_handler = SMTPHandler(
        mailhost=(cls.MAIL_SERVER, cls.MAIL_PORT),
        fromaddr=cls.FLASKY_MAIL_SENDER,
        toaddrs=[cls.FLASKY_ADMIN],
        subject=cls.FLASKY_MAIL_SUBJECT_PREFIX + ' Application Error',
        credentials=credentials,
        secure=secure)
    mail_handler.setLevel(logging.ERROR)
    app.logger.addHandler(mail_handler)
```

Recall that all configuration instances have a `init_app()` static method that is invoked by `create_app()`. In the implementation of this method for the `ProductionConfig` class, the application logger is configured to log errors to an email logger.

The logging level of the email logger is set to `logging.ERROR`, so only severe problems are sent by email. Messages logged on lesser levels can be logged to a file, syslog, or any other supported method by adding the proper logging handlers. The logging method to use for these messages largely depends on the hosting platform.

 If you have cloned the application's Git repository on GitHub, you can run `git checkout 17b` to check out this version of the application.

Cloud Deployment

The latest trend in application hosting is to host in the "cloud." This technology, which is formally known as Platform as a Service (PaaS), frees the application developer from the mundane tasks of installing and maintaining the hardware and software platforms on which the application runs. In the PaaS model, a service provider offers a fully managed platform in which applications can run. The application developer uses tools and libraries from the provider to integrate the application with the platform. The application is then uploaded to the servers maintained by the provider and usually is deployed within seconds. Most PaaS providers offer ways to dynamically "scale" the application by adding or removing servers as necessary to keep up with the number of requests received.

Cloud deployments offer great flexibility and are relatively simple to set up, but of course all that goodness comes at a price. Heroku, one of the most popular PaaS providers that offers very good support for Python, is studied in detail in the following section.

The Heroku Platform

Heroku was one of the first PaaS providers, having been in business since 2007. The Heroku platform is very flexible and supports a long list of programming languages. To deploy an application to Heroku, the developer uses Git to push the application to Heroku's own Git server. On the server the `git push` command automatically triggers the installation, configuration, and deployment.

Heroku uses units of computing called *dynos* to measure usage and charge for the service. The most common type of dyno is the *web dyno*, which represents a web server instance. An application can increase its request handling capacity by using more web dynos. The other type of dyno is the *worker dyno*, which is used to perform background jobs or other support tasks.

The platform provides a large number of plug-ins and add-ons for databases, email support, and many other services. The following sections expand on some of the details involved in deploying Flasky to Heroku.

Preparing the Application

To work with Heroku, the application must be hosted in a Git repository. If you are working with an application that is hosted on a remote Git server such as GitHub or BitBucket, cloning the application will create a local Git repository that is perfect to use with Heroku. If the application isn't already hosted on a Git repository, one must be created for it on your development machine.

 If you plan on hosting your application on Heroku, it is a good idea to start using Git from the very beginning. GitHub has installation and setup guides for the three major operating systems in their help guide (*http://help.github.com*).

Creating a Heroku account

You must create an account with Heroku (*http://heroku.com*) before you can use the service. You can sign up and host applications at the lowest service tier at no cost, so this is a great platform to experiment with.

Installing the Heroku Toolbelt

The most convenient way to manage your Heroku applications is through the Heroku Toolbelt (*https://toolbelt.heroku.com/*) command-line utilities. The Toolbelt is composed of two Heroku applications:

- `heroku`: The Heroku client, used to create and manage applications
- `foreman`: A tool that can simulate the Heroku environment on your own computer for testing

Note that if you don't have a Git client installed already, the Toolbelt installer also installs Git for you.

The Heroku client utility has to have your Heroku account credentials before it connect to the service. The `heroku login` command takes care of this:

```
$ heroku login
Enter your Heroku credentials.
Email: <your-email-address>
Password (typing will be hidden): <your-password>
Uploading ssh public key .../id_rsa.pub
```

 It is important that your SSH public key is uploaded to Heroku, as this is what enables the `git push` command. Normally the `login` command creates and uploads a SSH public key automatically, but the `heroku keys:add` command can be used to upload your public key separately from the login command or if you need to upload additional keys.

Creating an application

The next step is to create an application using the Heroku client. To do this, first make sure your application is under Git source control and then run the following command from the top-level directory:

```
$ heroku create <appname>
Creating <appname>... done, stack is cedar
http://<appname>.herokuapp.com/ | git@heroku.com:<appname>.git
Git remote heroku added
```

Heroku application names must be unique, so find a name that is not taken by any other application. As indicated by the output of the `create` command, once deployed the application will be available at *http://<appname>.herokuapp.com*. Custom domain names can also be attached to the application.

As part of the application creation, Heroku allocates a Git server: *git@heroku.com:<appname>.git*. The `create` command adds this server to your local Git repository as a `git` `remote` with the name `heroku`.

Provisioning a database

Heroku supports Postgres databases as an add-on. A small database of up to 10,000 rows can be added to an application at no cost:

```
$ heroku addons:add heroku-postgresql:dev
Adding heroku-postgresql:dev on <appname>... done, v3 (free)
Attached as HEROKU_POSTGRESQL_BROWN_URL
Database has been created and is available
 ! This database is empty. If upgrading, you can transfer
 ! data from another database with pgbackups:restore.
Use `heroku addons:docs heroku-postgresql:dev` to view documentation.
```

The HEROKU_POSTGRESQL_BROWN_URL reference is for the name of the environment variable that has the database URL. Note that when you try this, you may get a color other than brown. Heroku supports multiple databases per application, with each getting a different color in the URL. A database can be promoted and that exposes its URL in a DATABASE_URL environment variable. The following command promotes the brown database created previously to primary:

```
$ heroku pg:promote HEROKU_POSTGRESQL_BROWN_URL
Promoting HEROKU_POSTGRESQL_BROWN_URL to DATABASE_URL... done
```

The format of the DATABASE_URL environment variable is exactly what SQLAlchemy expects. Recall that the *config.py* script uses the value of DATABASE_URL if it is defined, so the connection to the Postgres database will now work automatically.

Configuring logging

Logging of fatal errors by email was added earlier, but in addition to that it is very important to configure logging of lesser message categories. A good example of this type of message are the warnings for slow database queries added in Chapter 16.

With Heroku, logs must be written to stdout or stderr. The logging output is captured and made accessible through the Heroku client with the heroku logs command.

The logging configuration can be added to the ProductionConfig class in its init_app() static method, but since this type of logging is specific to Heroku, a new configuration can be created specifically for that platform, leaving ProductionConfig as a baseline configuration for different types of production platforms. The HerokuConfig class is shown in Example 17-3.

Example 17-3. config.py: Heroku configuration

```
class HerokuConfig(ProductionConfig):
    @classmethod
    def init_app(cls, app):
        ProductionConfig.init_app(app)

        # log to stderr
        import logging
        from logging import StreamHandler
        file_handler = StreamHandler()
        file_handler.setLevel(logging.WARNING)
        app.logger.addHandler(file_handler)
```

When the application is executed by Heroku, it needs to know that this is the configuration that needs to be used. The application instance created in *manage.py* uses the FLASK_CONFIG environment variable to know what configuration to use, so this variable needs to be set in the Heroku environment. Environment variables are set using the Heroku client's config:set command:

```
$ heroku config:set FLASK_CONFIG=heroku
Setting config vars and restarting <appname>... done, v4
FLASK_CONFIG: heroku
```

Configuring email

Heroku does not provide a SMTP server, so an external server must be configured. There are several third-party add-ons that integrate production-ready email sending support with Heroku, but for testing and evaluation purposes it is sufficient to use the default Gmail configuration inherited from the base Config class.

Because it can be a security risk to embed login credentials directly in the script, the username and password to access the Gmail SMTP server are provided as environment variables:

```
$ heroku config:set MAIL_USERNAME=<your-gmail-username>
$ heroku config:set MAIL_PASSWORD=<your-gmail-password>
```

Running a production web server

Heroku does not provide a web server for the applications it hosts. Instead, it expects applications to start their own servers and listen on the port number set in environment variable PORT.

The development web server that comes with Flask will perform very poorly because it was not designed to run in a production environment. Two production-ready web servers that work well with Flask applications are Gunicorn (*http://gunicorn.org/*) and uWSGI (*http://bit.ly/uwsgi-proj*).

To test the Heroku configuration locally, it is a good idea to install the web server in the virtual environment. For example, Gunicorn is installed as follows:

```
(venv) $ pip install gunicorn
```

To run the application under Gunicorn, use the following command:

```
(venv) $ gunicorn manage:app
2013-12-03 09:52:10 [14363] [INFO] Starting gunicorn 18.0
2013-12-03 09:52:10 [14363] [INFO] Listening at: http://127.0.0.1:8000 (14363)
2013-12-03 09:52:10 [14363] [INFO] Using worker: sync
2013-12-03 09:52:10 [14368] [INFO] Booting worker with pid: 14368
```

The `manage:app` argument indicates the package or module that defines the application to the left of the colon and the name of the application instance inside that package on the right. Note that Gunicorn uses port 8000 by default, not 5000 like Flask.

Adding a requirements file

Heroku loads package dependencies from a *requirements.txt* file stored in the top-level folder. All the dependencies in this file will be imported into a virtual environment created by Heroku as part of the deployment.

The Heroku requirements file must include all the common requirements for the production version of the application, the *psycopg2* package to enable Postgres database support, and the Gunicorn web server.

Example 17-4 shows an example requirements file.

Example 17-4. requirements.txt: Heroku requirements file

```
-r requirements/prod.txt
gunicorn==18.0
psycopg2==2.5.1
```

Adding a Procfile

Heroku needs to know what command to use to start the application. This command is given in a special file called the *Procfile*. This file must be included in the top-level folder of the application.

Example 17-5 shows the contents of this file.

Example 17-5. Procfile: Heroku Procfile

```
web: gunicorn manage:app
```

The format for the Procfile is very simple: in each line a task name is given, followed by a colon and then the command that runs the task. The task name `web` is special; it is recognized by Heroku as the task that starts the web server. Heroku will give this task a `PORT` environment variable set to the port on which the application needs to listen for requests. Gunicorn by default honors the `PORT` variable if it is set, so there is no need to include it in the startup command.

> Applications can declare additional tasks with names other than `web` in the Procfile. These can be other services needed by the application. Heroku launches all the tasks listed in the Procfile when the application is deployed.

Testing with Foreman

The Heroku Toolbelt includes a second utility called *Foreman*, used to run the application locally through the Procfile for testing purposes. The environment variables such as FLASK_CONFIG that are set through the Heroku client are available only on the Heroku servers, so they also must be defined locally so that the testing environment under Foreman is similar. Foreman looks for these environment variables in a file named *.env* in the top-level directory of the application. For example, the *.env* file can contain the following variables:

```
FLASK_CONFIG=heroku
MAIL_USERNAME=<your-username>
MAIL_PASSWORD=<your-password>
```

 Because the *.env* file contains passwords and other sensitive account information, it should never be added to the Git repository.

Foreman has several options, but the main two are foreman run and foreman start. The run command can be used to run arbitrary commands under the environment of the application and is perfect to run the deploy command that the application uses to create the database:

```
(venv) $ foreman run python manage.py deploy
```

The start command reads the Procfile and executes all the tasks in it:

```
(venv) $ foreman start
22:55:08 web.1  | started with pid 4246
22:55:08 web.1  | 2013-12-03 22:55:08 [4249] [INFO] Starting gunicorn 18.0
22:55:08 web.1  | 2013-12-03 22:55:08 [4249] [INFO] Listening at: http://...
22:55:08 web.1  | 2013-12-03 22:55:08 [4249] [INFO] Using worker: sync
22:55:08 web.1  | 2013-12-03 22:55:08 [4254] [INFO] Booting worker with pid: 4254
```

Foreman consolidates the logging output of all the tasks started and dumps it to the console, with each line prefixed with a timestamp and the task name.

It is possible to simulate multiple dynos using the -c option. For example, the following command starts three web workers, each listening on a different port:

```
(venv) $ foreman start -c web=3
```

Enabling Secure HTTP with Flask-SSLify

When the user logs in to the application by submitting a username and a password in a web form, these values can be intercepted during travel by a third party, as discussed several times before. To prevent user credentials from being stolen in this way, it is necessary to use secure HTTP, which encrypts all the communications between clients and the server using public key cryptography.

Heroku makes all applications that are accessed on the *herokuapp.com* domain available on both *http://* and *https://* without any configuration using Heroku's own SSL certificate. The only necessary action is for the application to intercept any requests sent to the *http://* interface and redirect them to *https://*, and this is what the extension Flask-SSLify does.

The extension needs to be added to the *requirements.txt* file. The code in Example 17-6 is used to activate the extension.

Example 17-6. app/__init__.py: Redirect all requests to secure HTTP

```
def create_app(config_name):
    # ...
    if not app.debug and not app.testing and not app.config['SSL_DISABLE']:
        from flask.ext.sslify import SSLify
        sslify = SSLify(app)
    # ...
```

Support for SSL needs to be enabled only in production mode, and only when the platform supports it. To make it easy to switch SSL on and off, a new configuration variable called SSL_DISABLE is added. The base Config class sets it to True, so that SSL is not used by default, and the class HerokuConfig overrides it. The implementation of this configuration variable is shown in Example 17-7.

Example 17-7. config.py: Configure the use of SSL

```
class Config:
    # ...
    SSL_DISABLE = True

class HerokuConfig(ProductionConfig):
    # ...
    SSL_DISABLE = bool(os.environ.get('SSL_DISABLE'))
```

The value of SSL_DISABLE in HerokuConfig is taken from an environment variable of the same name. If the environment variable is set to anything other than an empty string, the conversion to Boolean will return True, disabling SSL. If the environment variable does not exist or is set to an empty string, the conversion to Boolean will give a False value. To prevent SSL from being enabled when using Foreman, it is necessary to add SSL_DISABLE=1 to the *.env* file.

With these changes, the users will be forced to use the SSL server, but there is one more detail that needs to be handled to make the support complete. When using Heroku, clients do not connect to hosted applications directly but to a *reverse proxy server* that redirects requests into the applications. In this type of setup, only the proxy server runs in SSL mode; the applications receive all requests from the proxy server without SSL because there is no need to use strong security for requests that are internal to the Heroku network. This is a problem when the application needs to generate absolute URLs that match the security of the request, because `request.is_secure` will always be `False` when a reverse proxy server is used.

An example of when this becomes a problem is the generation of avatar URLs. If you recall from Chapter 10, the `gravatar()` method of the `User` model that generates the Gravatar URLs checks `request.is_secure` to generate the secure or nonsecure version of the URL. Generating a nonsecure avatar when the page was requested over SSL would cause some browsers to display a security warning to the user, so all components of a page must have matching security.

Proxy servers pass information that describes the original request from the client to the redirected web servers through custom HTTP headers, so it is possible to determine whether the user is communicating with the application over SSL by looking at these. Werkzeug provides a WSGI *middleware* that checks the custom headers from the proxy server and updates the request object accordingly so that, for example, `request.is_secure` reflects the security of the request that the client sent to the reverse proxy server and not the request that the proxy server sent to the application. Example 17-8 shows how to add the `ProxyFix` middleware to the application.

Example 17-8. config.py: Support for proxy servers

```
class HerokuConfig(ProductionConfig):
    # ...
    @classmethod
    def init_app(cls, app):
        # ...

        # handle proxy server headers
        from werkzeug.contrib.fixers import ProxyFix
        app.wsgi_app = ProxyFix(app.wsgi_app)
```

The middleware is added in the initialization method for the Heroku configuration. WSGI middlewares such as `ProxyFix` are added by wrapping the WSGI application. When a request comes, the middlewares get a chance to inspect the environment and make changes before the request is processed. The `ProxyFix` middleware is necessary not only for Heroku but in any deployment that uses a reverse proxy server.

 If you have cloned the application's Git repository on GitHub, you can run `git checkout 17c` to check out this version of the application. To ensure that you have all the dependencies installed, also run `pip install -r requirements.txt`.

Deploying with git push

The final step in the process is to upload the application to the Heroku servers. Make sure that all the changes are commited to the local Git repository and then use git push heroku master to upload the application to the heroku remote:

```
$ git push heroku master
Counting objects: 645, done.
Delta compression using up to 8 threads.
Compressing objects: 100% (315/315), done.
Writing objects: 100% (645/645), 95.52 KiB, done.
Total 645 (delta 369), reused 457 (delta 288)

.---> Python app detected
.----> No runtime.txt provided; assuming python-2.7.4.
.----> Preparing Python runtime (python-2.7.4)
...
-----> Compiled slug size: 32.8MB
-----> Launching... done, v8
       http://<appname>.herokuapp.com deployed to Heroku

To git@heroku.com:<appname>.git
 * [new branch]      master -> master
```

The application is now deployed and running, but it is not going to work correctly because the deploy command was not executed. The Heroku client can run this command as follows:

```
$ heroku run python manage.py deploy
Running `python manage.py predeploy` attached to terminal... up, run.8449
INFO [alembic.migration] Context impl PostgresqlImpl.
INFO [alembic.migration] Will assume transactional DDL.
...
```

After the database tables are created and configured, the application can be restarted so that it starts cleanly:

```
$ heroku restart
Restarting dynos... done
```

The application shoud now be fully deployed and online at *https://<appname>.herokuapp.com*.

Reviewing Logs

The logging output generated by the application is captured by Heroku. To view the contents of the log, use the logs command:

```
$ heroku logs
```

During testing it can also be convenient to tail the log file, which can be done as follows:

```
$ heroku logs -t
```

Deploying an Upgrade

When a Heroku application needs to be upgraded the same process needs to be repeated. After all the changes have been committed to the Git repository, the following commands perform an upgrade:

```
$ heroku maintenance:on
$ git push heroku master
$ heroku run python manage.py deploy
$ heroku restart
$ heroku maintenance:off
```

The `maintenance` option available on the Heroku client will take the application offline during the upgrade and will show a static page that informs users that the site will be coming back soon.

Traditional Hosting

The traditional hosting option involves buying or renting a server, either physical or virtual, and setting up all the required components on it yourself. This is typically less expensive than hosting in the cloud, but obviously much more laborious. The following sections will give you an idea of the work involved.

Server Setup

There are several administration tasks that must be performed on the server before it can host applications:

- Install a database server such as *MySQL* or *Postgres*. Using a *SQLite* database is also possible but is not recommended for a production server due to its many limitations.
- Install a Mail Transport Agent (MTA) such as *Sendmail* to send email out to users.
- Install a production-ready web server such as *Gunicorn* or *uWSGI*.
- Purchase, install, and configure a SSL certificate to enable secure HTTP.
- (Optional but highly recommended) Install a front-end reverse proxy web server such as *nginx* or *Apache*. This process will serve static files directly and will forward any other requests into the application's web server listening on a private port on *localhost*.

- Server hardening. This groups several tasks that have the goal of reducing vulnerabilities in the server such as installing firewalls, removing unused software and services, and so on.

Importing Environment Variables

Similarly to Heroku, an application running on a standalone server relies on certain settings such as database URL, email server credentials, and configuration name. These are stored in environment variables that must be imported before the application starts.

Because there is no Heroku or Foreman to import these variables, this task needs to be done by the application itself during startup. The short code block in Example 17-9 loads and parses a *.env* file similar to the one used with Foreman. This code can be added to the *manage.py* launch script before the application instance is created.

Example 17-9. manage.py: Import environment from .env file

```
if os.path.exists('.env'):
    print('Importing environment from .env...')
    for line in open('.env'):
        var = line.strip().split('=')
        if len(var) == 2:
            os.environ[var[0]] = var[1]
```

The *.env* file must contain at least the FLASK_CONFIG variable that selects the configuration to use.

Setting Up Logging

For Unix-based servers, logging can be sent the *syslog* daemon. A new configuration specific for Unix can be created as a subclass of ProductionConfig, as shown in Example 17-10.

Example 17-10. config.py: Unix example configuration

```
class UnixConfig(ProductionConfig):
    @classmethod
    def init_app(cls, app):
        ProductionConfig.init_app(app)

        # log to syslog
        import logging
        from logging.handlers import SysLogHandler
        syslog_handler = SysLogHandler()
        syslog_handler.setLevel(logging.WARNING)
        app.logger.addHandler(syslog_handler)
```

With this configuration, application logs will be written to */var/log/messages*. The syslog service can be configured to write a separate log file or to send the logs to a different machine if necessary.

 If you have cloned the application's Git repository on GitHub, you can run `git checkout 17d` to check out this version of the application.

## CHAPTER 18

Additional Resources

You are pretty much done with this book. Congratulations! I hope the topics that I have covered have given you a solid base to begin building your own applications with Flask. The code examples are open source and have a permissive license, so you are welcome to use as much of my code as you want to seed your projects, even if they are of a commercial nature. In this short final chapter, I want to give you a list of additional tips and resources that might be useful as you continue working with Flask.

Using an Integrated Development Environment (IDE)

Developing Flask applications in an integrated development environment (IDE) can be very convenient, since features such as code completion and an interactive debugger can speed up the coding process considerably. Some of the IDEs that work well with Flask are listed here:

- PyCharm (*http://bit.ly/py-charm*): Commercial IDE from JetBrains with Community (free) and Professional (paid) editions, both compatible with Flask applications. Available on Linux, Mac OS X, and Windows.

- PyDev (*http://pydev.org*): Open source IDE based on Eclipse. Available on Linux, Mac OS X, and Windows.

- Python Tools for Visual Studio (*http://pytools.codeplex.com/*): Free IDE built as an extension to Microsoft's Visual Studio environment. For Microsoft Windows only.

When configuring a Flask application to start under a debugger, add the `--passthrough-errors --no-reload` options to the `runserver` command. The first option disables the catching of errors by Flask so that exceptions thrown while a request is handled are sent all the way up to the debugger. The second disables the reloader module, which confuses some debuggers.

Finding Flask Extensions

The examples in this book rely on several extensions and packages, but there are many more that are also useful and were not discussed. Following is a short list of some additional packages that are worth exploring:

- Flask-Babel (*http://bit.ly/fl-babel*): Internationalization and localization support
- Flask-RESTful (*http://bit.ly/fl-rest*): Tools for building RESTful APIs
- Celery (*http://bit.ly/celery-doc*): Task queue for processing background jobs
- Frozen-Flask (*http://bit.ly/flask-frozen*): Conversion of a Flask application to a static website
- Flask-DebugToolbar (*http://bit.ly/flask-debug*): In-browser debugging tools
- Flask-Assets (*http://bit.ly/fl-assets*): Merging, minifying, and compiling of CSS and JavaScript assets
- Flask-OAuth (*http://bit.ly/fl-oauth*): Authentication against OAuth providers
- Flask-OpenID (*http://bit.ly/fl-opID*): Authentication against OpenID providers
- Flask-WhooshAlchemy (*http://bit.ly/fl-whoosh*): Full-text search for Flask-SQLAlchemy models based on Whoosh (*http://pythonhosted.org//Whoosh/*)
- Flask-KVsession (*http://bit.ly/fl-kvses*): Alternative implementation of user sessions that use server-side storage

If the functionality that you need for your project is not covered by any of the extensions and packages mentioned in this book, then your first destination to look for additional extensions should be the official Flask Extension Registry (*http://bit.ly/fl-exreg*). Other good places to search are the Python Package Index (*http://pypi.python.org*), GitHub (*http://github.com*), and BitBucket (*http://bitbucket.org*).

Getting Involved with Flask

Flask would not be as awesome without the work done by its community of developers. As you are now becoming part of this community and benefiting from the work of so many volunteers, you should consider finding a way to give something back. Here are some ideas to help you get started:

- Review the documentation for Flask or your favorite related project and submit corrections or improvements.
- Translate the documentation to a new language.
- Answer questions on Q&A sites such as Stack Overflow (*http://stackoverflow.com*).
- Talk about your work with your peers at user group meetings or conferences.
- Contribute bug fixes or improvements to packages that you use.
- Write new Flask extensions and release them as open source.
- Release your applications as open source.

I hope you decide to volunteer in one of these ways or any others that are meaningful to you. If you do, thank you!

Index

Symbols

.env file, 223, 228

A

application programming interfaces (APIs)
    resources, 188
    versioning, 178
authentication, 181, 184

C

cloud, 217
code coverage, 197
configuration, 211, 216, 228

D

database
    association table, 150
    filter_by query filter, 159
    join query filter, 159
    joins, 158
    migrations, 64
    NoSQL, 50
    performance, 211
    relational model, 49
    relationships, 56, 61, 149, 166
    SQL, 49
debugging, 216

decorators, 115

E

email, 221
error handling, 180

F

Flask, 3
    abort function, 16, 180
    add_url_route function, 14
    after_app_request hook, 211
    application factory function, 78
    app_errorhandler decorator, 80, 180
    before_app_request hook, 107
    before_request hook, 15, 183
    blueprints, 79, 92, 179
    configuration object, 78
    context processors, 63, 116
    contexts, 12, 84
    cookies, 161
    current_app context variable, 13, 84
    debug argument, 9
    dynamic routes, 8
    errorhandler decorator, 29, 79, 80, 188
    extension registry, 232
    flash function, 46
    Flask class, 7
    flask.ext namespace, 17, 26

We'd like to hear your suggestions for improving our indexes. Send email to index@oreilly.com.

About the Author

Miguel Grinberg has over 25 years of experience as a software engineer. At work, he leads a team of engineers that develop video software for the broadcast industry. He has a blog (*http://blog.miguelgrinberg.com*) where he writes about a variety of topics including web development, robotics, photography, and the occasional movie review. He lives in Portland, Oregon with his wife, four kids, two dogs, and a cat.

Colophon

The animal on the cover of *Flask Web Development* is a Pyrenean Mastiff (a breed of *Canis lupus familiaris*). These giant Spanish dogs are descended from an ancient livestock guardian dog called the Molossus, which was bred by the Greeks and Romans and is now extinct. However, this ancestor is known to have played a role in the creation of many breeds that are common today, such as the Rottweiler, Great Dane, Newfoundland, and Cane Corso. Pyrenean Mastiffs have only been recognized as a pure breed since 1977, and the Pyrenean Mastiff Club of America is working to promote these dogs as pets in the United States.

After the Spanish Civil War, the population of Pyrenean Mastiffs in their native homeland plummeted, and the breed only survived due to the dedicated work of a few scattered breeders throughout the country. The modern gene pool for Pyreneans stems from this postwar population, making them prone to genetic diseases like hip dysplasia. Today, responsible owners make sure their dogs are tested for diseases and x-rayed to look for hip abnormalities before being bred.

Adult male Pyrenean Mastiffs can reach upwards of 200 pounds when fully grown, so owning this dog requires a commitment to good training and plenty of outdoors time. Despite their size and history as hunters of bears and wolves, the Pyrenean has a very calm temperament and is an excellent family dog. They can be relied upon to take care of children and protect the home, while at the same time being docile with other dogs. With proper socialization and strong leadership, Pyrenean Mastiffs thrive in a home environment and will provide an excellent guardian and companion.

The cover image is from Wood's *Animate Creation*. The cover fonts are URW Typewriter and Guardian Sans. The text font is Adobe Minion Pro; the heading font is Adobe Myriad Condensed; and the code font is Dalton Maag's Ubuntu Mono.

Get even more for your money.

Join the O'Reilly Community, and register the O'Reilly books you own. It's free, and you'll get:

- $4.99 ebook upgrade offer
- 40% upgrade offer on O'Reilly print books
- Membership discounts on books and events
- Free lifetime updates to ebooks and videos
- Multiple ebook formats, DRM FREE
- Participation in the O'Reilly community
- Newsletters
- Account management
- 100% Satisfaction Guarantee

Signing up is easy:

1. **Go to: oreilly.com/go/register**
2. **Create an O'Reilly login.**
3. **Provide your address.**
4. **Register your books.**

Note: English-language books only

To order books online:
oreilly.com/store

For questions about products or an order:
orders@oreilly.com

To sign up to get topic-specific email announcements and/or news about upcoming books, conferences, special offers, and new technologies:
elists@oreilly.com

For technical questions about book content:
booktech@oreilly.com

To submit new book proposals to our editors:
proposals@oreilly.com

O'Reilly books are available in multiple DRM-free ebook formats. For more information:
oreilly.com/ebooks

Spreading the knowledge of innovators   oreilly.com

DISCARD

CPSIA information can be obtained at www.ICGtesting.com
Printed in the USA
BVOW10s0058020514

352089BV00003B/3/P

9 781449 372620